PRAISE FOR *NURSE BUR*

"*Nurse Burnout: Overcoming Stress in Nursing* is a handbook for every nurse, from student to seasoned, who has experienced the bone-deep fatigue and strain of nursing's work. This book will become a dog-eared tool for developing a research-based plan for nurses to transform the real stressors of their work into wellness and resilience. The authors incorporate the concepts of Just Culture, change, conflict, and organizational milieu, promoting education, leadership, and strategies for physical, mental, spiritual, and emotional wellbeing in order to help nurses proactively develop healthy skills so they can continue to care for and heal others."

–Ruth Hansten, PhD, MBA, RN, FACHE
Founder & CEO
Hansten Healthcare, PLLC
www.Hansten.com & www.RROHC.com

"Suzanne Waddill-Goad demonstrates the esteem the public holds for nurses and their commitment to patient care. As technology and reimbursement continue to change, it places more pressure on nurses to provide quality nursing care and at the same time exceed the expectations of the patient and family. As noted, nurses face life and death situations every day and know that they must provide error free care in a pressurized environment. For this reason, it is imperative that nurses work in an environment where team work is the norm and everyone supports each other. Nurses rarely say no to anyone; they always think: I do one more thing; I can handle it. They do need self-care, time-out, and support from leadership. This book provides good insights about every day stress with practical examples highlighting the need to care for one's self and offering the tools to accomplish it."

–Suzanne Richins, RN, MBA, DHA, FACHE
Senior Vice-President for Healthcare
Global Targeting, Inc.

"Suzanne Waddill-Goad, in Nurse Burnout: Overcoming Stress in Nursing, wrote an excellent resource for nursing leaders and nursing managers seeking to better understand stress, fatigue, and burnout in our profession. The "Practice Pearls" are wonderful summary statements on knowledge, attitude, and skill development to promote individual and organizational health. Use of these interventions may promote improved patient outcomes as nurses strive to become more mindful and engaged as role-models of health in the workplace."

–Tona Leiker, PhD, APRN-CNS, CNE
Associate Professor, Nursing
Assistant Dean, Nursing Curriculum and Assessment
Nursing Programs, American Sentinel University

NURSE BURNOUT

combating stress in nursing

SUZANNE WADDILL-GOAD, DNP, MBA, RN, CEN

Sigma Theta Tau International
Honor Society of Nursing®

The Honor Society of Nursing, Sigma Theta Tau International (STTI) is a nonprofit organization founded in 1922 whose mission is to support the learning, knowledge, and professional development of nurses committed to making a difference in health worldwide. Members include practicing nurses, instructors, researchers, policymakers, entrepreneurs, and others. STTI's nearly 500 chapters are located at 695 institutions of higher education throughout Armenia, Australia, Botswana, Brazil, Canada, Colombia, England, Ghana, Hong Kong, Japan, Kenya, Lebanon, Malawi, Mexico, the Netherlands, Pakistan, Portugal, Singapore, South Africa, South Korea, Swaziland, Sweden, Taiwan, Tanzania, Thailand, the United Kingdom, and the United States of America. More information about STTI can be found online at www.nursingsociety.org.

Sigma Theta Tau International
550 West North Street
Indianapolis, IN, USA 46202

To order additional books, buy in bulk, or order for corporate use, contact Nursing Knowledge International at 888.NKI.4YOU (888.654.4968/US and Canada) or +1.317.634.8171 (outside US and Canada).

To request a review copy for course adoption, email solutions@nursingknowledge.org or call 888. NKI.4YOU (888.654.4968/US and Canada) or +1.317.634.8171 (outside US and Canada).

To request author information, or for speaker or other media requests, contact Marketing, Honor Society of Nursing, Sigma Theta Tau International at 888.634.7575 (US and Canada) or +1.317.634.8171 (outside US and Canada).

ISBN: 9781938835889
EPUB ISBN: 9781938835896
PDF ISBN: 9781938835902
MOBI ISBN: 9781938835919

Library of Congress Cataloging-in-Publication data

Names: Waddill-Goad, Suzanne, author. | Sigma Theta Tau International, issuing body.
Title: Nurse burnout : combating stress in nursing / Suzanne Waddill-Goad.
Description: Indianapolis, IN : Sigma Theta Tau International, [2016] | Includes bibliographical references.
Identifiers: LCCN 2015044715 (print) | LCCN 2015045429 (ebook) | ISBN 9781938835889 (alk. paper) | ISBN 9781938835896 (epub) | ISBN 9781938835902 (Pdf) | ISBN 9781938835919 (Mobi) | ISBN 9781938835896 (Epub) | ISBN 9781938835919 (Mobi)
Subjects: | MESH: Burnout, Professional--psychology. | Nurses--psychology. | Nursing. | Professional Competence.
Classification: LCC RT42 (print) | LCC RT42 (ebook) | NLM WY 87 | DDC 610.73--dc23
LC record available at http://lccn.loc.gov/2015044715

First Printing, 2016

Publisher: Dustin Sullivan
Acquisitions Editor: Emily Hatch
Editorial Coordinator: Paula Jeffers
Cover Designer: Rebecca Batchelor
Interior Design/Layout: Rebecca Batchelor

Principal Book Editor: Carla Hall
Development and Project Editor: Kezia Endsley
Copy Editor: Erin Geile
Proofreader: Todd Lothery
Indexer: Larry D. Sweazy

DEDICATION

A Taoist proverb states, "No one can see their reflection in running water. It is only in still water that we can see." Likewise, my journey in nursing has caused me to be still and insightful on many occasions. It has only been when I stopped moving that I could "truly see."

This book is dedicated to all the many fine nurses, both past and present, whose influence has shaped who I am today as a nurse and as a person. Their influence has been invaluable. My professional travels have led me coast to coast in the United States, and I am grateful for the countless opportunities the profession of nursing has provided me.

ACKNOWLEDGMENTS

This book would not have been possible without three dedicated nurse colleagues who were committed to this project as contributors: Dr. Debra Buck, Dr. Rita Haxton, and Dr. Holly Langster. They are accomplished nurse leaders, had their own reasons for wanting to be involved, and made the final product better because of their expertise, perspective, and guidance.

My many family, friends, and colleagues provided unwavering support and encouragement to do this project. They knew by watching my journey from afar and having their own experiences with stress, fatigue, and burnout that this story needed to be told. Onward!

ABOUT THE AUTHOR

Suzanne Waddill-Goad, DNP, MBA, BSN, RN, CEN, is president and principal consultant of Suzanne M. Waddill-Goad & Company, Inc., and assistant professor for the College of Nursing at the University of Tennessee. She began her journey in healthcare nearly 40 years ago and has spent her entire professional career working solely in the healthcare industry. Before she became self-employed, she held positions in various healthcare settings as a respiratory therapy technician, medical records clerk, transcriptionist, staff nurse, charge nurse, nursing supervisor, director of quality improvement, clinical educator, operations improvement coordinator, and chief nursing officer/assistant administrator.

Waddill-Goad holds a bachelor of science in nursing from the University of Colorado, a master of business administration from City University of Seattle, and a doctor of nursing practice in executive leadership from American Sentinel University. Her clinical practice spanned two decades in critical care and emergency nursing. Her graduate study was focused in the areas of managerial and executive leadership. In addition, she holds an executive education certificate as a Black Belt in Lean Six Sigma from The Ohio State University Fisher College of Business and retains clinical certification in emergency nursing.

Waddill-Goad's consulting practice specializes in operational improvement and leadership development. During the last 13 years, she has assisted clients in multiple states to achieve operational improvements in leadership, quality, safety, regulatory compliance, risk reduction, finance, and customer service. She has demonstrated success in developing new programs and leading teams with innovative ideas to their intended targets.

Most recently, she has received an academic appointment as an assistant professor in the College of Nursing at the University of Tennessee. She has since worked on nursing program development and teaches in the collaborative Executive Education program focused on healthcare with the University of Tennessee Haslam College of Business.

Waddill-Goad currently resides in Knoxville, Tennessee, with her husband.

CONTRIBUTING AUTHORS

Debra Buck, DNP, MSN, RN, is a nursing faculty member at Kellogg Community College, Spring Arbor University, and Walden University. Buck began her nursing career directly out of high school, graduating with an associate degree from a local community college. She worked in critical care and the emergency department for 14 years, transitioning to home care. During her time in home care, she completed her BSN from the University of Michigan. After several years working in the community, Buck returned to the hospital setting as a nurse recruiter. During her tenure, she made the decision to obtain a master of science in nursing with the goal of teaching nursing. Prior to completing her MSN, Buck returned to the emergency department as a clinical manager. During her tenure as clinical manager, she was instrumental in the department's adoption of an electronic medical record as part of a hospital-wide initiative. After the completion of her MSN, Buck was approached by a colleague with an opportunity to teach at the BSN level for a local college. Developing the curriculum for a community nursing course launched her career in the world of academia. After she began teaching, the opportunity arose to become the director of student health services for a local liberal arts college. This position allowed Buck to better accommodate her teaching schedule while becoming immersed in the college life. Buck made the decision to obtain a DNP in executive leadership to allow her the opportunity to teach at all levels. She completed her degree in 2014. Since completion of her degree, she has been teaching at the ADN, BSN, and MSN levels. She teaches courses such as nursing ethics, leadership, health policy, nursing research methods, community nursing, and medical informatics at the undergraduate and graduate levels. She is currently working with ADN students in the program she initially graduated from, teaching psychiatric nursing and leadership as well as teaching fundamentals in the clinical setting.

Rita Haxton, DNP, RN, NEA-BC, is vice president of Oncology and Inpatient Surgical Services for Baylor University Medical Center. She has focused the majority of her nursing career on nursing leadership. She has spent more than 20 years in an executive leadership position in both for-profit and non-profit community hospital environments. She received her BSN from Pittsburg State University, master in nursing from University of Missouri–Kansas City, and a doctorate of nursing practice-executive leadership from American Sentinel University in Aurora, Colorado. Haxton had experience in critical care and education prior to beginning her move into nursing leadership positions. She has presented on nursing management issues at regional and national conferences on such topics as emotional intelligence, positive work environment, generational issues, physician/nurse communication, and mental health. In addition, she has published articles in the *Journal of Healthcare Quality, Nursing Economics,* and *Quality Forum.* Her passion is patient-centered care and helping nurses find the area of nursing that ignites their passion. Haxton recently left her role as the chief nursing officer (CNO) of a 400-bed hospital to become the vice president of oncology and inpatient surgical services at Baylor University Medical Center in Dallas, Texas. She is most excited about the opportunity to use her experience in nursing leadership and her work with lean processes in a large community academic medical center.

Holly Jo Langster, DNP, FNP-C, HCA, CENP, is nursing project manager for Baptist Health Medical Center in North Little Rock, Arkansas. She's a small-town girl from central Illinois who selected nursing as a career 3 years after high school graduation. Although it took a few years to find the right career, it did not take any time at all to realize that nursing was more than a career choice. Langster thrives on challenge and new opportunities and loves project management, program development, and executive nursing leadership. The following experiences have contributed to her development: medical/surgical, emergency room, and cardiac nursing experiences as a registered nurse at Graham Hospital in Canton, Illinois. As a partner with medical director Dr. Gary Dunnington, Langster helped build the Breast Center at SIU in Springfield, Illinois. As a nurse practitioner, Langster learned the specialty practice of caring for and managing patients with a variety of breast diseases, including cancer. Administratively, Langster worked to ensure that the operations of the Breast Center were efficient and effective, and with the team approach to the fight against breast disease, the center eventually grew into the Cancer Institute of SIU. Nursing administration became a larger focus as Langster moved south to Arkansas and began working with the Baptist Health System, where 10 years in healthcare administration have expanded her exposure to hospital management and operations. Langster holds a doctor of nursing practice in executive leadership from American Sentinel University, a master in healthcare administration from Southern Illinois University, a master's degree in nursing as a family nurse practitioner from the University of Illinois-Chicago, a bachelor of science in nursing from Bradley University, and a nursing diploma from Methodist Medical School of Nursing. Langster is board certified as a family nurse practitioner and as an executive nursing leader. Her husband is an emergency room physician, and they have one child, Lucas. She is the daughter of an RN, the granddaughter of an LPN, and the great granddaughter of the town midwife.

TABLE OF CONTENTS

1 THE EFFECTS OF INHERENT STRESS 1

2 A SLICE OF REALITY 19

FOREWORD

Nurses are the fabric that holds the healthcare system together. Everyone has been touched by a nurse—from birth, through illness to wellness, and often even in death. Nurses are present during some of the most pivotal times in our lives.

Throughout my almost 30-year career, I have been privileged to meet hundreds of nurses and nurse leaders. Each of them reinforces a shared and basic value so many of us feel as we enter healthcare—the desire to serve others and make a difference in their lives. Keeping that basic motivation, nurtured throughout a long career in a way that energizes you, is what Suzanne Waddill-Goad delivers in *Nurse Burnout: Overcoming Stress in Nursing*.

Waddill-Goad is one of the outstanding nurse leaders I have been fortunate to work with. She has been a friend and colleague for many years and has devoted numerous days and nights to caring for a few of our hospitals during turbulent times. Her book, *Nurse Burnout,* proves to be not only an exceptional guide for nurses at every stage of their career but also a collection of practical wisdom to combat stress, fatigue, and burnout.

Nurse Burnout is more than a survival guide: The book is a timely perspective on dealing with stress during an era of fast-paced, technology-driven healthcare; increased regulations; emphasis on outcome metrics; and increased presence of violence in our society, which is spilling over into healthcare settings. This makes each strategy for dealing with stress more important than ever. Every student or practicing nurse—and in fact, all caregivers and leaders alike—will identify with the stressors described by Waddill-Goad.

On a personal note, Anna was one of those amazing nurses; she was my mom's hospice nurse. Anna connected with Mom in ways that seemed impossible for our family. Anna's grace, professionalism, and intuition led my mother through a chaotic and stressful journey. It was her final battle with cancer. She helped Mom find a path forward through a myriad of confusing choices. Anna's calm and clear communication, combined with her understanding of my mother's physical and emotional condition, made the difference. It was clear that Anna found joy in caring for patients and aiding in the comfort of a dying woman. It was core to why she was a nurse. I cannot imagine how my mother's last few weeks would have changed if Anna had suffered from stress, fatigue, or burnout.

Protecting the values that attracted so many to serve the sick and vulnerable must become a priority. That is what *Nurse Burnout* aims to deliver. The book will serve as a source of wisdom to many, including experienced nurses like Anna, and to countless new nurses as well as seasoned leaders. Enjoy.

–Grant Davies
CEO Hospitals, Valley Area
Sutter Health
Sacramento, California

INTRODUCTION

NURSING: AN ALTRUISTIC ENDEAVOR

Why write a book about nursing in relation to stress, fatigue, and burn-out? Experience—honestly, some has been good and some not so good. The author and the contributors have over 100 years of collective prac-tice experience. The truth needs to be told—the good, the bad, and the sometimes ugly. Overall, would each of the writers in this book choose nursing all over again? Absolutely!

Nursing is a fabulous career choice—it offers diversity, flexibility, entrepreneurism, innovation, a true sense of satisfaction, and a nice lifestyle. Nurses are generally people who exhibit traits of caring, nurturing, and altruism. They are good people to be around. Although the writers' journeys have been diverse, their reasons for becoming a nurse are very similar—to help others. Today, they each serve in different roles: One is a consultant, one is an educator, one is a nurse leader, and one is a project manager. They work in assorted environments, but their mission is still the same—to help others.

The good thing is helping others never gets old. What does wear on a nurse's psyche is the environment. Adverse stimuli can be both internal and external: regulatory and policy changes, leadership influences, operational initiatives, industry mandates, customer expectations, publicly reported data, quality metrics, colleague relationships, and the list goes on. This book explores those influences and discusses how those influences affect stress, fatigue, and burnout. The most important offerings from this book (the "Practice Pearls") are suggested strategies for fresh thinking, ways to harness and manage overwhelming stress (to prevent reaching burnout), and ways to set new priorities to care for yourself.

Nurses need to be encouraged to prioritize self-care and recovery time to promote their own health and well-being. Both the brain and body need downtime for optimal performance. Stress and fatigue affect safety and quality; we can no longer push ourselves to the brink. We need "renewable" energy to be at our personal and professional best; we need to be mindful and think intentionally; and we need to perform with the best interest of ourselves as well as others.

STRESS, FATIGUE, AND BURNOUT IN NURSING

What is causing nurses stress? The American Holistic Nursing Association (2015) lists staffing (or the lack thereof), schedules (rotating), long shifts (often back to back), fatigue (both mental and physical), excessive noise in the workplace, workload (too much to do), time pressures (not enough time to get the work done), difficult colleagues (teamwork or the lack of), supervisors (not qualified for the role and/or not supportive of staff needs), challenging patients and families (sicker patients and families with unrealistic expectations), a lack of control in the work environment (mandates driven by others), role conflict, ambiguity, inadequate resources of all types, floating to new work areas with little or no orientation, underuse of talent, exposure to toxic substances, and the potential to experience hostility or violence (by patients, visitors, or co-workers), to name a few. Although this is not an exhaustive list of the challenges nurses face, it a fairly comprehensive list of what might qualify as daily stressors in the work environment.

Why are nurses burning out? Three out of four nurses cited the effects of stress and overwork as a top health concern in a 2011 survey by the American Nurses Association (ANA); the ANA attributed problems of fatigue and burnout to what seems to be a chronic nursing shortage

(ANA, 2011). Recent research has found nurses working shifts longer than 8 to 9 hours were two-and-a-half times more likely to experience burnout (Gupta, 2015). A 2012 study by Stimpfel, Sloan, and Aiken revealed that nurses underestimate their own recovery time from long, intense clinical engagements and that consolidating challenging work into shorter time frames may not be a sustainable strategy to attain work-life balance.

In addition, researchers at the University of Akron (Dill and Erickson) found in 2014 that nurses who are primarily motivated by the desire to help others, rather than enjoyment of work, were more likely to burn out (American Sociological Association, 2014). Could we be our own worst enemies? Should education and awareness about the potential for burnout begin in formal nursing training? Should selection criteria to become a nurse include an assessment for motivation and the potential to burn out?

Nurses are qualitative experts; we are constantly gathering information on a daily basis. What we have not been quite as good at is collecting formal data, analyzing it, and sharing evidence in our practice environments. If nurses were able to use the information they collect more effectively, or on a real-time basis, could it decrease the potential for burnout? If nurses were allowed more autonomy in role design, assessing job fit, and analyzing systems affecting their work, and given training for optimal interpersonal relationships, it is plausible that burnout could be lessened and maybe entirely avoided.

In addition, what are the responsibilities of nurses and nurse leaders collaboratively in relation to stress, fatigue, and burnout in nursing?

PRACTICE PEARLS

- Know the signs and most common causes of burnout.
- Design or improve systems known to cause stress.
- Create a campaign of cultural awareness regarding the risks of burnout.

WHY CHOOSE NURSING?

Nursing is more than a job. It is a profession that attracts those who value compassion and want to do greater good in the world. Many say it is a calling because it provides a platform for making a difference in other people's lives. The wide range of experiences that nurses encounter from birth to death can be both painful and joyous.

The profession of nursing provides endless options to practice in a variety of healthcare settings. A career in nursing provides the flexibility to choose from an array of options different from most other career choices. Nursing allows you to enter and exit the profession, work more or less than full-time, work in non-traditional settings, have around-the-clock hours, and have fluid movement among types of healthcare milieus and patient populations.

The practice of nursing offers ample time during a lifelong career to learn new skills for advancement. A multitude of possibilities exists for a non-linear career track in various areas of specialty practice. Additionally, a variety of educational options exists for continual learning. Educational opportunities include both formal and informal course work. This array of choices is appealing to many choosing a first or alternate career. And the choice of a career in nursing often allows a planned or intentional approach to work-life balance.

Nursing is both art and science; the profession has the capacity to capture a person's soul by experiences that may be singular in nature or combined physical, mental, emotional, and spiritual encounters. Many of these encounters will leave a lasting impression. They will not only shape a nurse's professional practice journey but can also add positive value to a nurse's life as a whole.

Traditional nursing practices are founded in science. Evidence-based care and compensable quality metrics are changing the practice of nursing. While nurses have always been concerned about patient outcomes, responsibility has escalated and now accountability lies in the hands of those providing direct care.

Nursing leaders' contributions to direct care are appropriate educational preparation and the obligation to provide or ensure available resources— the people, space, supplies, and equipment for optimal care delivery. As the healthcare environment has become more fiscally challenged, this is often much more complicated that it appears. Staffing shortages, drug recalls, equipment back orders, and space challenges often inhibit smooth transitions of care and efficient work processes. The resulting stress for nurse leaders can be overwhelming, as job expectations have drastically changed in recent years.

While nurses are qualified to use their ability to influence others' choices about health promotion and treatment of illness, they also need to care for themselves. They are often viewed by the public as experts and are the most revered profession with the highest levels of perceived honesty and ethical standards (Riffkin, 2014). This standing in the public eye provides a respected voice to lead the future of healthcare, and nurses must lead first by example.

A change in thinking is required; the old-style thinking of treatment of illness needs to be replaced with mindful health. Part of being mindful relative to health is prevention of illness and an intention to be healthy. Actions speak louder than words. No change ever comes from continuing on the same path—good, bad, or otherwise.

Nursing also provides a stage to observe a variety of ethnic and cultural practices firsthand. Nurses play an important part in assisting others through challenging health and psychosocial situations. The profession offers exceptional but often testing circumstances to be thoughtfully navigated on a daily basis. Boredom is seldom used to describe a day in a nurse's life. Each day offers a distinct experience, generally in the presence of newly introduced people.

The number of nurses in the United States is estimated to be just short of 3 million (Bureau of Labor Statistics, 2012). Nursing is the fastest-growing occupation in the United States and is expected to grow an additional 22%, adding more than 581,000 jobs by 2018 (Johnson & Johnson, 2015). These growth projections for the future have been based on an aging population and an aging of the current nursing workforce. A comprehensive report can be found here:

> http://bhpr.hrsa.gov/healthworkforce/reports/
> nursingworkforce/nursingworkforcefullreport.pdf

The median income for nursing, stated to be $65,470, is higher than most other professions, and the nursing profession can be entered with minimal academic preparation of an associate degree (Bureau of Labor Statistics, 2012). As described in the Bureau of Labor Statistics *Occupational Outlook Handbook* (2012), the outpatient arena of healthcare encounters has grown, with technological advancement over recent years creating a shift in the traditional hospital-type acute care setting. This shift has expanded the non-acute care choices for a multitude of new career options. The outpatient setting also offers a number of other benefits, including more traditional work hours without required weekend and holiday commitments.

PRACTICE PEARLS

- Nursing provides a flexible and rewarding career.
- Nurses have the ability to make a stable living wage.
- Nurses have many opportunities to continue learning and to change practice among specialties.

ADVANCES IN TECHNOLOGY

While the process of nursing has essentially remained the same for centuries, the practice of care delivery has changed significantly in recent decades. Research advances in medical care and treatment delivery have spurred new technology essentially focused on automation. Much of the healthcare delivery system can be or is sequenced and repetitive. This has facilitated the creation and use of new medical devices improving safety and driving more precise, predictable outcomes. Examples include robotic surgery, high-tech implantable devices, newly developed pharmaceuticals, smart technology for medical equipment such as infusion pumps, as well as many others.

Meaningful use certified electronic health records, driven by the Centers for Medicare & Medicaid Services (CMS), are being implemented in a variety of stages in an effort to improve patient care (CMS, 2014). The implementation of meaningful use with electronic medical or health records (EMR or EHR) is tied to a vision for improvement in information access and retrieval, as well as health-provider ties to financial incentives. The improvement in access to timely medical information for emergent situations, or as people are transient and mobile in today's society, will benefit both patients and their caregivers by having the necessary information available to allow the best, informed choices for their care.

Electronic access to information for nurses to make care decisions for patients is essential (Kelley, Brandon, & Docherty, 2011). A multitude of nursing publishers has made traditional texts, policies, procedures, and diagnostic tools immediately available via electronic means. This real-time information accessibility assists nurses in making sound care decisions for their assigned patient population.

The advent of social media has presented benefits and challenges for the nursing and healthcare industries. The immediacy of information is a benefit; however, the commitment to confidentiality and privacy can often be challenging (National Council of State Boards of Nursing [NCSBN], 2011). Most organizations set policy regarding the use of social media, appropriate cell-phone usage, and photography with a strict set of parameters not to be violated (for patient privacy) without adverse consequences. Nurses must use extreme caution not to breach the trust of patient relationships and confidentiality of patient-related health information.

PRACTICE PEARLS

- Nurses must be technologically savvy.
- Nurses need to know the law and policy about patient privacy and confidentiality.
- Social media should only be used to improve patient access to appropriate information.

THE PACE OF CHANGE

One of the most memorable recurring dreams nurses have in common goes like this:

> "The shift was very busy and I spent the entire time running from room to room doing assessments, vital signs, giving medications, and doing minor procedures. I barely had time to take a break or finish my documentation before the shift was nearing its end. It was a tough day with provider and family challenges. I really felt I had too many sick patients to adequately care for, but it was almost time for the end of the shift report to the oncoming nurse. Whew—I had survived! Then, at the end of the shift report, the oncoming nurse asked me about Patient X. I politely told her I was not assigned Patient X. She looked surprised, so we verified the daily assignments for each nurse per the assignment sheet. And, there it was in plain black and white—Patient X was assigned to me. Oh, no! Would they still be alive since I had not seen them all shift? They had missed all of their medications, assessments, and vital signs. How could nobody have known? Did the charge nurse not go in and check on the patient when rounding? Did the patient not have any clinical needs or diagnostic testing that required consultation with a nurse?" And, then the dreaming nurse wakes up from the nightmare!

Nursing is a fast-paced, evolving profession. Nurses experience a great deal of stress and must adapt to change with grace. Nielsen and Munir (2009) posited that the ability to effectively adapt to change shows tenacity and courage. Nurses are courageous individuals and can be persistent when necessary. The industry needs courageous leaders, at all levels, now more than ever to lead the way to a better system of healthcare in the United States.

INTRODUCTION

The speed of life and work has increased exponentially, as described by Kotter (2011), who questioned whether people are really able to keep up with the new pace. The norm is no longer status quo; change comes at a rapid and unrelenting speed. Keeping up with the new pace of information, life, and change is difficult. Most likely it will even be more so in the future. Technology will continue to drive the pace of change as improvements promise to enhance productivity, allowing nurses to do more with less or in the same amount of time. Could technology be another source of nurses' stress? Is the digital age really making people more productive?

By 2020, there will be five generations of nurses in the workforce. At present, the four generations working bring differing expectations for their personal and professional lives (Putre, 2013). This diversity can provide a number of organizational challenges to current work process and business operations. Unintentional interpersonal conflict can result due to different styles of communication, expectations, and frames of reference.

In general, younger generations are more familiar with technology and are used to a faster pace of life. This is all they have known and it is their "normal." For those who are older, human contact has always been valuable; they are learning new technology and being introduced to the importance of work-life balance. Understanding the vast differences in preferences and expectations of each generation will be crucial for healthcare organizations of the future. One size won't fit all. In addition, the aging of the U.S. population has tremendous implications for the healthcare industry, both as employers of an aging workforce and as providers of services to a growing number of older patients (Harrington & Heidcamp, 2013). Who will fill the vacancies? We know younger workers do not want or expect the same things from their work. Will older workers feel compelled to stay in the workforce?

Time is finite; more time cannot be created. Thus, we have to think intentionally about how time should be spent. Could we decrease stress by spending less time in stress-invoking environments, or could the environments be made less stress-invoking? Both might be true. Because nurses cannot change the pace, they must be willing to change themselves.

PRACTICE PEARLS

- Understand what you can and cannot control in your environment to alleviate stress.

- Thoughts, feelings, and actions are connected. Be mindful about how you think and feel.

- You need to care for yourself first in order to be the best caregiver for others.

THE EFFECTS OF STRESS

Numerous studies, both in and outside of healthcare, have analyzed the effects of stress. In addition to reduced job satisfaction, stressed or fatigued workers can suffer health consequences, are more apt to make mistakes, are often unable to sleep and rest effectively, are absent from work more often, and experience a host of psychosocial distress, as described by Waddill-Goad in 2013. The new corporate business model of healthcare has fueled a dilemma for many nurses and other healthcare workers. Contemporary business practices and politics in healthcare have led to commercial value systems being instilled into professions that have been traditionally considered moral practice involving care and compassion (Roberts, Grubb, & Grosch, 2012). The strain has produced more stress for caregivers in an already stress-laden environment.

A multitude of studies has shown that nurses have a propensity for burnout. The very nature of caring for others, sometimes without the ability to set limits (of time, compassion, etc.), potentiates the possibility for burnout. Articles found in the scholarly literature cite up to a prevalence of 40% of people feeling stressed and having the potential to become burned out in the workforce. Because burnout is known to result in physical, mental, and social consequences, why is it not more commonly discussed and addressed, and why aren't actions taken to prevent it? Is it an ignored phenomenon? Not only does burnout have personal consequences, but there are also organizational concerns that all relate to the bottom line, such as retention and turnover, employee satisfaction, clinical outcomes, medical errors, and patient satisfaction. The Bureau of Labor Statistics ranked nurses fifth of all occupations in 2010 in the number of workdays missed due to occupational injuries and illness (ANA, 2011).

Because stress, fatigue, and burnout have serious penalties for both individuals and organizations, the healthcare industry must take note. Effective awareness and reduction approaches must be considered and implemented in the healthcare work environment. The potential for violence and incivility on the part of patients, visitors, and healthcare workers must not be tolerated. Integrated job stress and other health and safety interventions targeted to the needs of nurses and their work settings will facilitate the overarching goal of improving health and safety (Roberts et al., 2012). In turn, this will lead to safer and better patient care.

PRACTICE PEARLS

- Recognize stress and its consequences.
- Attempt early intervention to mitigate stress.
- Adopt healthy coping strategies for stress tolerance.

REFERENCES

American Holistic Nurses Association. (2015). *Holistic stress management for nurses.* Retrieved from http://www.ahna.org/Resources/Stress-Management

American Nurses Association (ANA). (2011). *2011 ANA health & safety survey: Hazards of the RN work environment.* Retrieved from http://www.nursingworld. org/2011HealthSurveyResults.aspx

American Sociological Association. (2014, August 19). Nurses driven mainly by a desire to help others are more likely to burn out. *Science Daily.* Retrieved from www.sciencedaily.com/releases/2014/08/140819082918.htm

Bureau of Labor Statistics. (2012). *Occupational outlook handbook: Registered nurses.* Retrieved from http://www.bls.gov/ooh/healthcare/registered-nurses.htm

Centers for Medicare & Medicaid Services (CMS). (2014, October 6). *2014 Definition stage 1 of meaningful use.* Retrieved from https://www.healthit.gov/ providers-professionals/meaningful-use-definition-objectives

Gupta, S. (2015, September 14). Why America's nurses are burning out. *Everyday Health Media, LLC.* Retrieved from http://www.everydayhealth.com/news/why-americas-nurses-are-burning-out/

Harrington, L. & Heidcamp, M. (2013, March). The aging workforce: challenges for the healthcare industry workforce. *Issue Brief, the NTAR Leadership Center.* Retrieved from http://www.dol.gov/odep/pdf/ NTAR-AgingWorkforceHealthCare.pdf

Health Resources and Services Administration (HRSA). (2013, April). The U.S. nursing workforce: Trends in supply and education. *The U.S. Department of Health and Human Services.* Retrieved from http://bhpr.hrsa.gov/healthworkforce/reports/ nursingworkforce/nursingworkforcefullreport.pdf

Johnson & Johnson. (2015). *Why be a nurse?* The Campaign for Nursing's Future. Retrieved from http://www.discovernursing.com/why-be-a-nurse

Kelley, T. F., Brandon, D. H., & Docherty, S. L. (2011). Electronic nursing documentation as a strategy to improve quality of patient care [Abstract]. *Journal of Nursing Scholarship, 43*(2), 154–62.

Kotter, J. (2011, July 19). Can you handle an exponential rate of change? *Forbes.* Retrieved from http://www.forbes.com/sites/johnkotter/2011/07/19/can-you-handle-an-exponential-rate-of-change

National Council of State Boards of Nursing (NCSBN). (2011, November). *A nurse's guide to the use of social media.* Retrieved from https://www.ncsbn.org/NCSBN_ SocialMedia.pdf

Nielsen, K., & Munir, F. (2011). How do transformational leaders influence follower's affective well-being? Exploring the mediating role of self-efficacy. *Work & Stress, 23,* 313–329.

Putre, L. (2013). Generations in the workplace. *Hospital & Health Networks, 87*(1), 26–31.

Riffkin, R. (2014, December 18). Americans rate nurses highest on honesty, ethical standards. *Gallup.* Retrieved from http://www.gallup.com/poll/180260/americans-rate-nurses-highest-honesty-ethical-standards.aspx

Roberts, R., Grubb, P. L., & Grosch, J. W. (2012, June 25). Alleviating job stress in nurses. *Medscape.* Retrieved from http://www.medscape.com/viewarticle/765974

Stimpfel, A. W., Sloane, D. M., & Aiken, L. H. (2012). The longer the shifts for hospital nurses, the higher the levels of burnout and dissatisfaction. *Health Affairs, 31*(11), 2501–2509.

Waddill-Goad, S. (2013). *The development of a leadership fatigue questionnaire* (doctoral dissertation). American Sentinel University, Aurora, Colorado.

1

THE EFFECTS OF INHERENT STRESS

Suzanne Waddill-Goad, DNP, MBA, RN, CEN

OBJECTIVES

- Explore the stress-fatigue-burnout connection.

- Understand organizational stress.

- Understand the risks related to burnout.

- Define the health concerns resulting from stress, fatigue, and burnout.

- Define the practice considerations.

Nursing is an inherently stressful profession. Situations that nurses encounter on a regular basis are unimaginable to most people: life, death, and just about everything in between can be a "day in the life" of a nurse. Only recently have some of the experiences of nurses been profiled or highlighted by the media and television. Although these venues do not always provide the most factual information, they have certainly raised public awareness—both about choosing nursing as a profession and the impact to population health as a result of poor health choices.

THE REALITY OF NURSING AND STRESS

Stress at work is usually due to a number of intertwined issues, such as people issues, conflict, deadlines, job pressures, mundane tasks, and being overly committed. Nursing and healthcare are people businesses. Where there are people, there will be clashes in thinking, values, and beliefs. Nurses work with a variety of diverse types of people: different ethnic cultures, frames of reference, ages, faiths, and more. The neutrality nurses must exhibit is sometimes in itself stress-producing when conflict arises and is contrary to a nurse's own feelings or beliefs. Nurses regularly play the role of peacemaker in an ambiguous industry filled with extreme chaos and change.

Dr. Hans Seyle (1956) has been credited as the first scientist to identify stress as a concept. His work, which spanned decades beginning in the 1930s, identified stress as a difficult-to-define and subjective phenomenon. Nevertheless, it is well known and generally understood by most people that excessive stress leads to negative physical and emotional effects on the body and mind. Many other researchers have since studied the effects of stress on the human body, the resulting adaption or maladaptation, and the ensuing consequences of each type of stress (positive, negative, and neutral stress—called *eustress*). Nurses often feel stress secondary to the work environment—whether it is real or perceived.

Waddill-Goad (2013) noted previous research over a decade, including work by Wells (2011), who cited Harvey et al. (2009), as well as Mimura and Griffiths (2003), suggesting that healthcare workers experience significantly more stress in the workplace than the wider working population. Thus, nurses must learn to tolerate a certain level of inherent stress that will always exist to some degree in healthcare settings. The healthcare environment has become quite complex and increasingly chaotic due to regulatory mandates, external influences, and excessive industry change. Nurses must learn healthy skills to adapt to, effectively cope with, and adequately deflect and defuse the day-to-day stress in order to survive. By becoming successful at stress survival, nurses can enhance their own practice and satisfaction at work.

It is essential to recognize stress and the subsequent stressors before you progress to fatigue and burnout. Unfortunately, stress has a way of sneaking up on you in an insidious fashion. Sometimes before you know it, it is too late. It tends to come and go in irregular cycles or patterns, depending on life circumstances. Examples affecting the perception of stress include physical illness, injuries, mental exhaustion, fatigue, and attitudinal and/or behavior changes. Often, others recognize the warning signs before they become apparent to you. Loved ones and co-workers may recognize the signs before you do.

Before one reaches chronic fatigue and realizes there might be a problem, burnout may be just around the corner. Nurses are especially at risk because they are experts in "carrying on" despite challenging conditions. For example, in the emergency department, a nurse might see a patient with a minor malady, such as a strain or sprain of a muscle or joint, and in the adjacent room might be assigned to a patient with a major illness, such as a cardiac arrest or a serious traumatic injury. There is little time to process emotional or physical reactions predicated by stress. Stressful events, especially in this type of acute clinical environment, occur with some regularity. The inability to process the information leaves stress unchecked. That type of unresolved stress can layer upon previous experiences and progress over time from an acute issue to chronic fatigue and eventually lead to burnout.

PRACTICE PEARLS

- Recognize that the healthcare environment is chaotic, fraught with unpredictability, and can be inherently stressful.

- Limit the effects of uncontrollable environmental influences that may cause stress by identifying early warning signals: feeling overwhelmed, experiencing mental and/or physical fatigue, and a change in thinking (positive to negative). These can all be remedied by taking a break.

- Learn to be emotionally aware. Emotional intelligence and practicing self-control are key strategies to overcome the effects of stress.

THE PERSONAL STRESS–FATIGUE CONNECTION

In the 1940s, Forbes began writing about the symptoms of fatigue. He described it as strain from hurrying and worrying, emotional stress, and working to one's maximum capacity (Forbes, 1943). Fatigue produces nearly universal symptoms—people experience a similar feeling of "tiredness"—but the precipitating factors differ. The current dictionary definition of fatigue is "a weariness or exhaustion from exertion" (fatigue, n.d.).

While some people experience fatigue from an extreme or serious illness, others experience it due to normal activities of daily life. A number of populations have been studied in relation to fatigue via a variety of research experiences: those with a multitude of illness types, industry- or job-specific occupational classes, as well as the public at large. Occupational health researchers estimate that 10% to 40% of the general population experiences fatigue on a regular basis (Waddill-Goad, 2013).

It is well documented in the literature how the effects of stress and fatigue affect performance, skill, relationships, and health. Much of the research has been conducted outside of healthcare by the military, aviation, and nuclear industries; however, all of these industries, including healthcare, are considered to be high risk. Should we view nursing as a high-risk career? Is the risk of stress and its consequences taught in formal nursing educational settings? Is the risk well known and understood by the practicing population of nurses? The answer to all of these questions is not necessarily.

The North American Nursing Diagnosis Association (n.d.) defines *fatigue* as an overwhelming, sustained sense of exhaustion and decreased capacity for physical and mental work at the usual level. Fatigue is also described as acute or chronic, depending on the time frame it lasts and whether it succumbs to relieving factors. *Acute fatigue* is reversible and relieved by compensatory mechanisms; *chronic fatigue* is irreversible and impervious to compensation mechanisms (Beurskens et al., 2000).

Much of what has been studied and written about fatigue intertwines the two types—physical and mental fatigue may be difficult to separate and one might potentiate the other. Which comes first? Could stress be leading to fatigue, thus causing unsafe conditions in the workplace? Or is fatigue leading to stress, thus causing unsafe conditions in the workplace? Is mental fatigue primary or secondary to physical fatigue? Can they both directly affect brain function? These are important and daunting questions that need to be addressed.

A great deal of research exists relative to nurses and stress or fatigue for those working at the bedside. The occupational health industry has been concerned with fatigue as an unsafe malady in the workplace, and many think it is a risk that can be managed (Lerman et al., 2012). What about healthcare leaders? Are they aware of the consequences for themselves and the workforce they lead? Do leaders experience the same or similar symptoms? If so, what are the consequences to their leadership practice?

Frings's (2011) study concerned inflexible thinking by those who are fatigued in rapidly changing work surroundings. Healthcare is a rapidly changing work environment. If inflexible thinking occurs in a chaotic environment, it could hypothetically be dangerous or even lethal. Early signs of stress and fatigue could signal performance danger when quick thinking is required.

PRACTICE PEARLS

- Recognize the connection between stress and fatigue.
- When you're feeling the effects of either stress or fatigue, choose to break the cycle.
- Address the cause of your stress and fatigue early on to prevent progression.

ORGANIZATIONAL STRESS

The connections among stress, people, and organizations have been studied for decades. Most empirical studies of the connection between organizational stress and people blame discrepancies between human behavior and the organizational environment as the cause of stress (Edwards, 1992). Edwards (1992) suggested that this kind of stress stems from individuals' weaknesses in response to organizational stressors. Earlier, Lazarus and Folkman (1984) characterized stress as a process-based relationship, identifying three types of stress: positive, *eustress* (neutral), or *distress* (negative).

Lazarus and Folkman's transactional theory of stress and coping applies well to the nursing profession, because nursing is a process. These researchers characterized stress between a person and his or her work environment as a changing process. They also heavily emphasized coping as a key strategy for adaption and optimal health. Nurses are immersed in a changing environment and must learn adequate coping mechanisms due to continual exposure to a plethora of adverse experiences. The ability to recognize stress—in real time—and its impact in the work environment is key to optimal performance in thinking and subsequent action. The healthy or positive experiences aren't usually the ones that leave a lasting impression. It is the negative experiences of grief, pain, and loss that all manage to take a toll and are hard to forget.

Thus, effective coping is affected by *perception* (adequate or inadequate), *assessment* of the stressor (accurate or inaccurate), and *controllability* of the stressor (able or unable). What we think about becomes reality. Perception influences beliefs and behavior. If your ability to accurately perceive a situation or adequately assess stressors is compromised, your response to the stressor may be insufficient. Stress, fatigue, and burnout all negatively influence your ability to precisely perceive, assess, and respond to internal and external stressors.

PRACTICE PEARLS

- Work is only a small portion of your life. Treat it as such.
- Change the way you think to change your life.
- All encounters, whether positive or negative, can be optimally reframed as a growth experience.

THE RISK OF BURNOUT

Burnout first emerged as a social problem, not a scholarly construct. The concept was shaped by pragmatic practice rather than by academic concerns (Schaufeli, Maslach, & Marek, 1993). The study of burnout began in the 1970s as a result of a combination of personal and professional circumstances. Freudenberger (1974) coined the term "burnout," and measuring it has been a controversial issue ever since (Schaufeli & Van Dierendonck, 1993). Nearly simultaneously in the 1970s, those in research and practice began to study burnout. Researchers have since found that studying it is somewhat difficult, because fatigue leading to other symptoms and eventually to burnout can have vague and variable descriptions. As study progressed over two decades into the 1990s, the scholarly literature reported more than 100 physical and mental symptoms describing the phenomenon or concept of burnout.

The most widely used definition for *burnout* to date is from Maslach and Jackson (1981), who describe it as a syndrome of emotional exhaustion, depersonalization, and reduced personal accomplishment. More contemporary definitions (after virtually 35 years of study) now found in the literature include new wording relative to an erosion of engagement. *Engagement* is newer nomenclature relative to satisfaction and has been measured by surveys in healthcare for patients, providers, and employees in recent times. Unfortunately, burnout has been associated with working conditions in the nursing profession for some time (O'Mahony, 2011).

O'Mahony (2011) summarized the consequences of burnout (based on previous decades of research) as low morale; increased absenteeism from sickness; decreased effectiveness and productivity; poorer job performance and patient care; and higher staff turnover. With another impending nursing shortage on the horizon, and an increased need for health services due to the aging population, the profession cannot afford to lose well-educated and/or trained nurses. Nursing must change the culture of accepted stress, subsequent behavioral responses, and the stress-producing work environments. The risk of nurses burning out is just too high in the current systems for practice.

Little information exists relative to the consequences of burnout in the nursing leadership population. It is suspected that when nurse leaders reach the point of burnout in their chosen career path, they suddenly do one of the following: take a break, change specialties by returning to clinical practice, or may even quit nursing altogether. Numerous studies suggest nurse leaders are generally older than the average nurse due to the experience and expertise required by these roles (Waddill-Goad, 2013). In addition, nurse leaders may be more susceptible to fatigue secondary to stress-producing role demands. They often have high levels of responsibility and few limitations regarding the amount of time they spend at or doing work-related tasks. Each of these factors increases the risk of burnout.

A recent study, using an emergency nurse sample, cites support from one's nurse manager as one of the most influential drivers for nursing burnout (Hunsaker, Chen, Maughan, & Heaston, 2015). In addition, a correlation between burnout and turnover for intensive care unit (ICU) nurses was established (Shoorideh, Ashktorab, Yaghmaei, & Majd, 2015). Thus, burned out nurses will look for a change; both studies highlight the importance of nursing leaders knowing the symptoms of burnout, having a positive relationship with others, and especially forging a healthy bond between nurses and nurse leaders.

Henry (2014) described six areas prone to increase the potential for burnout in nurses; she adapted her conclusion of precursors to burnout from a previous study performed nearly a decade before by Maslach and Leiter in 2005:

- **Workload:** The amount of work to complete in a day and the frequency of surprising or unexpected events

- **Control:** Participation in decisions that affect the work environment and quality of leadership in upper management

- **Reward:** Recognition for achievement and opportunities for bonuses or raises

- **Community:** Frequency of supportive work interactions and close personal friendships at work

- **Fairness:** Management's dedication to giving everyone equal consideration; clear and open procedures for allocating rewards or promotion

- **Values:** Potential to contribute to the larger community and confidence that the organizational mission is meaningful

Each of Henry's (2014) described elements drive nurses to work excessively; skip meals and breaks; feel unappreciated, unrecognized, and unsupported by management; and experience cultures opposite to transparency, truth, and fairness. All of these examples may lead nurses in any professional role or setting to experience burnout.

PRACTICE PEARLS

- Learn to recognize the early symptoms that may lead to burnout.
- Find a work culture that fits your professional and personal values.
- Learn to value taking time to care for yourself.
- Know your mental, emotional, physical, and spiritual triggers before you hit your limit!

HEALTH CONCERNS RELATED TO STRESS AND WORKAHOLISM

Enlightened organizations have begun to take an interest in the abstract connections among mind, body, wellness, and health (Waddill-Goad, 2013). A healthy organizational workforce makes for a healthy organizational bottom line: fewer costs for consumption of healthcare; less absenteeism; lower vacancy rates; improved employee satisfaction with the work environment; better customer experiences; higher quality metrics; and satisfactory financial outcomes. Healthcare is a tough business requiring 24-hour per day and 7-day per week availability of adequate resources and highly trained personnel. The literature is rife with numerous examples citing health concerns relative to shift rotation and patterns of working off-shifts.

Nurses must begin to care for themselves, as they do others, by making their own good health and illness prevention a top priority. Not only will individual nurses benefit from the results, but their patients and associated organizations will as well. If nurses continue "business as usual" in their stress-laden work environments, their future individual health, career satisfaction, and success, as well as organizational outcomes, may all be at risk.

Nurses also have a strong tendency to become workaholics. Working fewer days with longer shifts allows nurses to take second jobs, work per diem, and pick up extra shifts in their primary place of employment. The definition of *workaholism* is to work compulsively at the expense of other pursuits (workaholism, n.d.). Interestingly, the organization called Workaholics Anonymous was formally started by a nurse in the early 1980s in California. At nearly the same time, in various locations across the world, people began to notice a pathological aspect to activity. They noticed that pathological activities, including work, were affecting them like other detrimental forms of addiction (Workaholics Anonymous, 2015).

The symptoms of workaholism include higher work-related stress and job burnout rates, anger, depression, anxiety, and other psychosomatic symptoms (Osterweil, n.d.). Most workaholics are in denial about their behavior and their condition, and they often wonder why others do not work as hard as they do. The hallmark characteristics of workaholism as identified by Workaholics Anonymous are:

- A strong internal drive in which work is a priority over other important things in life

- An inability to disengage or disconnect from work

- Working in excess of 40 hours per week on a routine basis

- Work negatively affecting relationships with family and friends due to obsession

- "Normal" practices are defined by routinely working while on vacation, while eating meals, on weekends, in bed, and while driving

While some of these characteristics may not be applicable to a clinical or bedside nurse's role, they certainly apply to a nursing leader or other healthcare leader's role. This definition and individual assessment should lead the industry to question if current work-related role expectations are healthy. Are healthcare workers setting a good example? Are healthcare leaders being good role models for others?

PRACTICE PEARLS

- Establish solid boundaries for hours of work, rest, and relaxation.

- Practice healthy habits: Engage in regular exercise; eat a balanced and healthy diet; get the recommended 8 to 9 hours of sleep per night; and take breaks when needed.

- Engage in positive coping strategies and change your current behavior. A few suggestions to decrease stress include talking about the stress, writing your thoughts and/or feelings in a journal, and taking regularly planned breaks from stressful conditions.

- Consider a planned "digital detox." Personal and professional technologic advances and the resulting 24/7 availability can be an overwhelming source of stress and can lead to technology fatigue. Examples include limiting or eliminating access while on vacation, limitations on days off, and less access during non-work periods throughout the day. Ask yourself the following question: "Do I really need to be available now?"

PRACTICE CONSIDERATIONS

Theories, conceptual frameworks, and models are not discovered; they are created and invented based on facts, observable evidence, and the originator's ingenuity in pulling facts together and making sense of them (Polit & Beck, 2012). Nursing needs a successful prescription to combat stress, fatigue, and burnout. Adaption and influence are known to affect performance (Waddill-Goad, 2013), and nurses need to learn how to compensate for stressful work environments.

An assessment—both individual and organizational—must be considered to identify stressors. Individuals must take responsibility and learn to assess the predictors or precursors of stress, fatigue, and

13

burnout. Organizations and individuals must share responsibility for the consequences of stress, fatigue, and burnout. The responsibility for organizational stress lies solely within healthcare entities. The leaders in healthcare need to become adept at assessing their own organizations relative to the potential for stress, fatigue, and burnout for themselves and for their workforce.

Changes to current practice, role responsibilities, organizational design, and workload must be carefully planned. Healthcare personnel need to be passionate about and feel energized from their work. The norm of feeling overwhelmed should no longer be accepted. A growing body of literature suggests that organizational leadership is closely associated with a variety of employee and organizational outcomes—the good and the bad (Kelloway & Barling, 2010). Leaders at all levels in healthcare must take note of the current state of affairs and be willing to look in the mirror to see if their influence requires a change in course. For example, charge nurses might evaluate how their assigned shift runs: Do their co-workers get scheduled breaks, are the patient assignments fair and equitable, and are they viewed by their peers as helpful and effective in the role?

Nursing has traditionally promoted individuals who demonstrate independence, clinical competence, and enhanced productivity (Kerfoot, 2013). In the future, traits such as a commitment to health and well-being should be equally considered. All nurse leaders must adopt effective strategies for positively coping with their own stressors and then convey those abilities to influence the workforce they lead.

Richards (2013, p. 94) questioned whether a "scattered and splattered attention and drive-by focus" in the haste to get more done is hardwiring caregivers for disaster. The pace of nursing and healthcare continues to escalate in both speed and intensity. Richards (2013) calls *wellpower* a learned nursing ability for self-assessment, recognition of stress, and positive correction to adapt to stressful conditions. Adaption is believed to preserve wellpower.

Today's nurses need wellpower. Nurses must also embrace a questioning attitude, one of rational inquiry. Instead of focusing on "how did things get to be this way?" (thinking in the past), a change in thinking such as "what could be done to improve the current situation?" (thinking in the present) could be very beneficial. Participating in change may reduce stress from change. Doing things the way we've always done them won't lead us to a better future. In fact, things could get a lot worse before they get better. The external changes in the healthcare industry are driving internal changes in practice. Rather than resisting change, embracing it and being a part of improvement can be energizing.

Caring is the core business of healthcare (Williams, McDowell, & Kautz, 2011), and nurses need to first care for themselves. We need to focus on wellness and well-being. We must design and implement effective methods to prevent or decrease the effects of stress, fatigue, and burnout.

CONCLUSION

This chapter provided an introduction to the timely topics of stress, fatigue, and burnout in nursing. Highlights provided a historical overview, relevant definitions, and real-life examples of how to decrease stress, the resulting fatigue, and the potential for burnout. While the environmental stressors may seem impervious to change, we can change ourselves and our response to them. However, this type of change is not easy. It will require a deeper awareness of the present circumstances, clear recognition of our stressors and their impact, and thoughtful action to achieve a different response. The next chapter will explore and connect challenges in the healthcare business environment to what nurses feel in their practice.

REFERENCES

Beurskens, A. J. H. M., Bultmann, U., Kant, I., Vercoulen, J. H. M. M., Bleijenberg, G., & Swaen, G. M. H. (2000). Fatigue among working people: Validity of a questionnaire measure. *Occupational Environmental Medicine, 57*(5), 353–357. doi: 10.1136/oem.57.5.353

Edwards, J. R. (1992). A cybernetic theory of stress, coping and well-being in organizations. *Academy of Management Review, 17*(2), 238–274.

fatigue. (n.d.). In *Merriam-Webster's online dictionary*. Retrieved from http://www.merriam-webster.com/dictionary/fatigue

Forbes, W. (1943). Problems arising in the study of fatigue. *Psychosomatic Medicine, 5,* 155–157.

Freudenberger, H. (1974). Staff burn-out. *Journal of Social Sciences, 30*(1), 159–165.

Frings, D. (2011, August 16). *Working together can help battle the effects of fatigue* [Press release]. Retrieved from https://www.apa.org/news/press/releases/2011/08/fatigue-effects.aspx

Henry, B. J. (2014). Nursing burnout interventions: What is being done? *Clinical Journal of Oncology Nursing, 18*(2), 211–214.

Hunsaker, S., Chen, H., Maughan, D., & Heaston, S. (2015). Factors that influence the development of compassion fatigue, burnout, and compassion satisfaction in emergency department nurses. *Journal of Nursing Scholarship, 47*(2), 186–194.

Kelloway, E. K., & Barling, J. (2010). Leadership development as an intervention in occupational health psychology. *Work & Stress, 24,* 260–279.

Kerfoot, K. M. (2013). Are you tired? Overcoming leadership styles that create leader fatigue. *Nursing Economics, 31*(3), 146–151.

Lazarus, R. S., & Folkman, S. (1984). *Stress, appraisal, and coping.* New York, NY: Springer.

Lerman, S. E., Eskin, E., Flower, D. J., George, E. C., Gerson, B., Hartenbaum, N., ... Moore-Ede, M. (2012). Fatigue risk management in the workplace. *Journal of Occupational and Environmental Medicine, 54*(2), 231–258.

Maslach, C., & Jackson, S. E. (1981). The measurement of experienced burnout. *Journal of Organizational Behavior, 2*(2), 99–113. doi: 10.1002/job.4030020205

North American Nursing Diagnosis Association (NANDA) Nursing Diagnoses. (n.d.). *Nursing diagnoses for fatigue.* Retrieved from http://nandanursingdiagnoses.blogspot.com/2011/11/nursing-diagnoses-for-fatigue.html

O'Mahony, N. (2011). Nurse burnout and the working environment. *Emergency Nurse, 19*(5), 30–37.

Osterweil, N. (n.d.). Are you a workaholic? *WebMD*. Retrieved from http://webmd. com/balance/features/are-you-a-workaholic

Polit, D. F., & Beck, C.T. (2012). *Nursing research: Generating and assessing evidence for nursing practice* (9th ed., Rev.). Philadelphia, PA: Wolters Kluwer; Lippincott, Williams & Wilkins.

Richards, K. (2013). Wellpower: The foundation of innovation. *Nursing Economics, 31*(2), 94–98.

Schaufeli, W. B., Maslach, C., & Marek, T. (Eds.). (1993). *Professional burnout: Recent developments in theory and research.* New York, NY: Taylor & Francis.

Schaufeli, W. B., & Van Dierendonck, D. (1993). The construct validity of two burn-out measures. *Journal of Organizational Behavior, 14*(7), 631–647. doi: 10.1002/job.4030140703

Seyle, H. (1956). *The stress of life* (1st ed.). New York, NY: McGraw-Hill.

Shoorideh, F. A., Ashktorab, T., Yaghmaei, F., & Majd, H. A. (2015). Relationship between ICU nurses' moral distress with burnout and anticipated turnover. *Nursing Ethics, 22*(1), 64–76. doi: 10.1177/0969733014534874

Waddill-Goad, S. (2013). *The development of a leadership fatigue questionnaire* (doctoral dissertation). American Sentinel University, Aurora, Colorado.

Williams, R. L., McDowell, J. B., & Kautz, D. D. (2011). A caring leadership model for nursing's future. *International Journal for Human Caring, 15*(1), 31–35.

Workaholics Anonymous. (2015). *The history of workaholics anonymous.* Retrieved from http://www.workaholics-anonymous.org/contact-us/about-w-a

workaholism. (n.d.). Retrieved from http://dictionary.reference.com/browse/workaholism

2

A SLICE OF REALITY

Suzanne Waddill-Goad, DNP, MBA, RN, CEN
Rita Haxton, DNP, RN, NEA-BC

OBJECTIVES

- Understand that healthcare is a business.

- Consider how organizational demands create stress.

- Explore how consumers affect the healthcare business.

- Explore how regulations affect the healthcare business.

- Consider how transitioning to practice can help new graduates deal with stress.

When a person makes the decision to seek a career in nursing, the most common reason is his or her innate desire to genuinely help people and care for them in times of need. The person must thrive on being challenged and enjoy the complexity of a difficult academic science curriculum. Many future nurses were inspired by a nurse they met who was a relative or friend. They might also have been a patient or were involved with someone who was seriously ill. They might have had the opportunity to admire the skill, dedication, and passion of the nurses who cared for their family or friend.

The business side of healthcare is usually not one of the reasons why a person chooses to become a nurse. It is vitally important as a nursing professional to remember that healthcare is a business. The business of healthcare is complex and challenging; it will impact all nurses' jobs in almost every area of nursing they might encounter in their career. Every person in the United States and throughout the world feels the cost of healthcare. The cost of healthcare in the United States has slowed in growth over the past 4 years, but the percentage of national spending on healthcare in 2012 was still 17.2% (Mangan, 2014).

Healthcare is big business. Nurses have the ability to influence much of what transpires in the industry. As an informed and responsible member of the healthcare team, nurses need to perform at a higher level than ever before. They also need to be informed about the result of their decision-making. Stress, fatigue, and burnout can affect a nurse's ability to optimally perform his or her job. Not understanding how these factors affect the cost of healthcare and truly influence patient outcomes can be extremely detrimental—both to the nurses and their organizations.

UNDERSTANDING THE BUSINESS OF HEALTHCARE

Healthcare is changing, and the days of "business as usual" are over. Many of healthcare's old systems simply do not work in the current environment. Healthcare in the United States, in every aspect, is struggling with rising costs, reduced reimbursement by both government and private insurance providers, and a continual push to improve the quality of care for well-informed and demanding patients. For several years, both healthcare leaders and government policy-makers have tried numerous ways to reduce the cost of healthcare while improving the quality. The focus has been on improving patient safety by reducing errors, educating the public to be better healthcare consumers, forcing healthcare institutions to move to an electronic medical or health record, and increasing the investment in people whose sole focus is to identify and prevent medical fraud.

In the past, healthcare has been a supply-driven system organized around how physicians practice (Porter & Lee, 2013). The movement toward a patient-centered system focused on the needs of patients is the path of the future. How does healthcare change a currently fragmented physician-driven system to a value-based healthcare system?

The patient-centered movement began with the 2006 book *Redefining Health Care*, by Michael Porter and Elizabeth Teisberg. The authors first introduced a value agenda. Porter and Teisberg set forth a "vision for the healthcare system where everything in the system is aligned around its fundamental purpose—patient health" (2006, p. 381). This unique vision painted a different picture of a future healthcare system. The key initiatives were integration strategies that increased value to the patient, rather than just increasing volume.

To create this new healthcare system, these authors described how all healthcare clinical professionals, leaders, insurance companies, governmental leaders, technology developers, and pharmaceutical companies must look at what they are doing to improve value for the patient. In addition, they must be sure the service they provide is available to all patients equally (Porter & Teisberg, 2006).

PRACTICE PEARLS

- Identify and eliminate process or system waste in your workplace.
- Be involved in staff councils to affect practice decisions.
- Caring and compassion are the heart of nursing; be a patient advocate and the communication link to other healthcare disciplines.
- Patients trust nurses; nurses are the best people to discuss their fears and concerns.

ORGANIZATIONAL DEMANDS: PILLARS, METRICS, AND TARGETS

Healthcare is a very data-intensive business. In recent years, most organizations have adopted a cache of tools from general business models to track, trend, and compare outcomes. The generic example in Table 2.1 shows how a system of "pillars"—each a specific aspect of a business—can be displayed with measurable goals, targets, results, and action plans for course correction.

TABLE 2.1 SYSTEM OF PILLARS WITH MEASURABLE GOALS AND TARGETS

XYZ Valley Community Hospital, Departmental Strategic Plan Supporting Performance and Quality Improvement Measures					
90-Day Action Plans	Target	June	July	August	Corrective Action
Service					
Finance					
People					
Quality					
Growth					

Healthcare organizations providing inpatient and/or outpatient care have designated quality measures that must be reported to a national database and to the Centers for Medicare & Medicaid Services (CMS). Many organizations also have to report quality measures to private insurance agencies to meet contractual arrangements or for reimbursement purposes. The majority of the measures are focused on clinical care.

Healthcare systems provide this information to the agencies in multiple ways. As the increased use of electronic medical or health records has expanded in hospitals and clinics, the electronic record must have the ability to retrieve data via reports from patient care documentation. If the reports cannot be retrieved from an electronic system, the data must be collected manually. The organization's leadership has a responsibility to designate staff who review and report the required patient-related data to the requesting entity.

The importance of compliance with reporting of accurate quality metrics has been heightened. Reimbursement incentives are now connected to the results of the measurable quality metrics collected by healthcare organizations. Patient outcome data has become a top priority in most healthcare organizations' agendas.

The reimbursement for Medicare patients has changed from a volume-based fee-for-service system to a value-based payment system. Participating hospitals are paid for inpatient acute care services based on the quality of care, not just the quantity of the services provided. This is an extreme change in historical industry practice, affecting all aspects of healthcare: strategic planning, organizational performance, clinicians practice patterns, and financial outcomes. Hence, it is imperative for nurses to understand how comprehensive, accurate, and timely clinical documentation impacts a cascade of events in the overall organizational system.

Congress authorized Inpatient Hospital Value Based Purchasing (VBP) as a part of the Affordable Care Act (Centers for Medicare & Medicaid Services [CMS], 2012). Each year, a percentage of the Diagnosis Related Group (DRG) payment received for the care of a Medicare patient is withheld from the DRG payment by Medicare. This percentage is held until the results of the quality metrics are reported and finalized.

Hospitals whose results fall below the benchmark do not receive the withheld percentage, and hospitals that exceed the benchmark receive a value-based bonus payment. The percentage of payment withheld has increased each year in order to push hospitals to continue improving the required set of quality measures, thus improving patient outcomes. Under the current VBP system, the percentage withheld is being escalated and will reach a maximum of 2% in 2017 and is expected to remain at that level going forward (CMS, 2014).

The governmental quality measures have been changing every year since the creation of the quality program. In the beginning, the metrics were related to the percentage of times a recognized evidence-based process guideline was implemented. In the first 2 years, the clinical process measures were valued at 70%, and the patient experience measure was valued at 30%. As organizations performed better (rates reached 98%–100%), the bar was raised to no longer measure processes but instead to measure patient outcomes. In 2015, the four quality domains measured were: 1) clinical process of care, 2) patient experience of care, 3) outcome, and 4) efficiency (CMS, 2014).

For 2015, CMS cited the VBP metrics as follows:

- **Clinical process of care:** 13 measures with a value weight of 20%

- **Patient experience:** 8 measures with a value weight of 30%

- **Outcome:** 5 measures with a value of 30%

- **Efficiency:** 1 measure with a value of 20%

As the process and patient outcomes for disease hit the desired quality targets, measures will be changed to other disease categories requiring improvement. The challenge for the healthcare industry is to push forward toward better patient outcomes across all disease states while reducing cost and expanding patients' access to care.

Nurses are responsible for the majority of patient care; they can influence and have the ability to improve a large percentage of these clinical measures when given the appropriate environment and resources to do so. In the clinical process category of metrics, nurses can affect the measures by ensuring orders are processed correctly and that a particular process occurs on time. In the patient experience measures, nursing directly affects seven of the eight measures. In addition, nurses have a unique ability to facilitate communication between the medical provider and the patient.

In the area of outcomes, nurses make a difference through the use of critical communication in the event of a changing patient condition. In the measure of efficiency, the importance of nursing assessment and patient evaluation is key. Nurses must determine if patients clearly understand their discharge instructions to prevent an adverse outcome or readmission. The efficiency metric is measured by the analysis in a window of time: spending from inpatient and outpatient healthcare encounters over a 33-day period (CMS, 2014).

PRACTICE PEARLS

Nursing-sensitive indicators impact the quality of care:

- Focus on the assessment and care of skin integrity to prevent hospital-acquired pressure ulcers.
- Focus on the prevention of patient falls.
- Always wash your hands to prevent the potential spread of infection.
- Ambulate patients early and often; bed rest often delays recovery.
- Remove urinary catheters as soon as possible.
- Nurses have the ability to influence patient experience: Be a reliable communication conduit for the patient, family, and clinicians.
- Patient education is crucial for appropriate follow-up care. Use teach-back to assess whether patients understand their care plan.

A review by CMS of the results of 25 CMS quality-reporting programs from 2006 to 2013 showed significant progress in care improvement and cost reduction for Medicare patients. Of the 119 publicly reported performance rates, 95% showed progress, and 35% of the 119 measures exceeded the 90% metric of success (Earl, 2015). The CMS deputy administrator for innovation and quality/chief medical officer, Patrick Conway, reported the nation has made clear progress in improving healthcare by achieving the three aims: 1) better care, 2) smarter spending, and 3) healthier people (Earl, 2015).

Positive improvements resulting from the push by governmental quality organizations and insurance companies for outstanding quality metrics will result in the continued refinement and expansion of the program. It is predicted that new quality metrics will replace the old and be measured and reported in all areas of healthcare. It is essential for nurses to become familiar with these quality metrics and become comfortable with others viewing their documentation and measurable practice outcomes. For experienced nurses, this may be somewhat disconcerting and a source of stress. Nursing care is now under a spotlight and being showcased—good, bad, or otherwise.

The intention of this government intervention is good. CMS is using the quality metrics as a lever to transform the delivery of healthcare. The focus has been with the Medicare population, but it is likely all Americans will receive a collateral benefit from this quality measurement program. Healthcare professionals have become immersed in system reform and engaged in clinical and outcome improvement, and they are striving for results to achieve better care in a better system.

CONSUMER INFLUENCES IN HEALTHCARE

With increased access to the Internet, healthcare consumers are better educated. They are able to stay better informed about the healthcare industry and the latest trends than at any previous time in history. Today's consumers are demanding healthcare systems and experiences that accommodate their busy schedules, provide useful information that can be obtained quickly and easily, and allow them to be involved in decision-making. These consumers are different from those in the past because they also demand better access to care and better communication and participation with their healthcare providers. Plans of treatment are often devised jointly and executed via creative methods.

One of the most controversial changes in healthcare is a greater shift in cost to the consumer. As companies who do provide health insurance for their employees change the coverage and benefit plans, it requires a change in consumer behavior regarding access and consumption. Many Americans have viewed healthcare access and treatment as a right; however, it has become a costly privilege. This change has made consumers more conscientious about their healthcare decisions (Mangan, 2014).

Healthcare organizations have also been affected by these industry changes; more of the cost of benefits has been passed along to employees in healthcare, causing a new financial strain. A common cycle of stress is outlined here:

Change → Stress Perceived As Negative → Adverse Consequences

Healthcare providers who understand the nuances of demand consumerism and its influence on the marketplace will thrive. The impact of better quality and outcomes secondary to tuned-in healthcare providers and patients will facilitate the shift from an illness-based focus to a system of prevention. Healthcare costs will decrease, and the population at large will be healthier. It could be as simple as, it's all in how you look at it (change). A new view of change producing stress is outlined here:

Change → Positively Viewed Stress → New Ideas for System Improvement

A future challenge to healthcare organizations, as well as clinicians, will be to understand the interplay between internal and external customers. Those outside of healthcare are driving much of the industry change (especially, those who pay for it). They now expect higher quality at a more reasonable cost. It will be necessary to develop better ways of proactively working with suppliers of healthcare to accommodate changing demands of the modern consumer. Many of the systems in healthcare have been designed by and for the providers, not the payers or consumers. As this changes, the modern consumer will expect immediate access, accurate communication, and collegial collaboration among all types of team members in an expedient fashion.

Modern consumers want to ask difficult questions about their care and treatment plans. They expect nearly immediate answers. The healthcare system's ability to satisfy consumer demand for convenience, access, and timely information will have a significant impact on where consumers take their business. Consumers will decide with whom and where to receive care, giving thought to quality, outcomes, and the entity's overall success in the delivery approach to healthcare.

THE INFLUENCE OF REGULATION

A large portion of the U.S. population is covered by federal or state agencies in order to gain access to healthcare. It is unusual to find a healthcare provider or agency that does not accept patients covered by a government-sponsored program. Thus, the majority of all healthcare agencies must meet the regulatory standards and requirements of CMS. An online manual of regulations is regularly published to allow easy access for clientele. To ensure regulations are followed, most state agencies have been engaged in the monitoring process.

The surveyors may make announced or unannounced visits to healthcare sites. Visits may be prompted by consumer complaints related to care and treatment, access, or any other alleged violation in the regulations. Routine reviews of quality data are commonplace. Reviews are required to determine if the quality of services meets professionally recognized standards of practice in healthcare (CMS, 2013).

Nursing is affected by regulations and compliance requirements. Generally, staff nurses are somewhat unaware of the monumental amount of guidelines that must be followed. A number of references have been provided in this chapter for access and review of a multitude of healthcare entity requirements. Organizations are influenced by federal and state regulations, accrediting organizations such as The Joint Commission, and payers. The decision to be surveyed by The Joint Commission is a voluntary choice by an organization. If the organization does choose to be surveyed by an accrediting organization such as The Joint Commission, the organization will have deemed status with CMS if it receives accreditation. If an organization chooses not to seek accreditation with an approved regulatory body, CMS will independently survey the organization approximately every 3 years.

Healthcare accrediting agencies' purpose is to collaborate with and evaluate healthcare entities against a set of recognized, industry-specific standards to ensure quality and safety for the public. A 2009 Industry Relations and Government Relations Committee comparative of the top three accrediting agencies' similarities and differences can be found at https://www.namss.org/Portals/0/Regulatory/The%20Big%20 Three%20A%20Side%20by%20Side%20Matrix%20Comparing%20 Hospital%20Accrediting%20Agencies.pdf.

Most organizations build compliance with regulations into their strategic plan executed via daily operations. Activities include safety checks, surveillance, and visual observation of work processes. Surveys are becoming more frequent, and real-time readiness is crucial.

Figure 2.1 illustrates one approach to reach successful organizational outcomes.

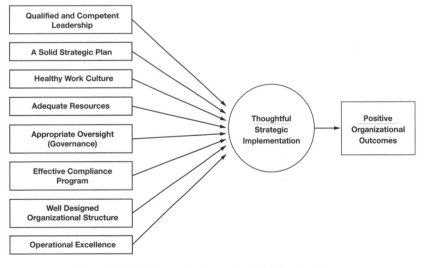

Figure 2.1   Organizational model for success.

For example, the applicable standards for compliance with CMS are similar to The Joint Commission regulations. Nursing is a key participant in survey activity. The majority of healthcare operations includes areas of regulations focusing on patient care standards, infection control, medication administration, care coordination, patient safety, environment of care, and life safety. The process for The Joint Commission standard development occurs with input from healthcare professionals, providers, subject-matter experts, consumers, government agencies (including the Centers for Medicare & Medicaid Services), and employers. After the standards are proposed using scientific literature and expert consensus, they are reviewed by the board of commissioners. For a new standard to be added, it must meet certain criteria—it must be related to patient safety or quality of care, have a positive impact on health outcomes, meet or surpass laws and/or regulations, and have the ability to be accurately and readily measured (The Joint Commission, 2015).

TRANSITION-TO-PRACTICE PROGRAMS FOR NEW GRADUATES

"A determined effort to focus new nurses on the positive aspects of the nursing profession can successfully extinguish a great deal of the negativity that new graduates often feel, and can promote a smoother transition into practice." (Dyess & Sherman, 2009, p. 409)

In recent years, the National Council of State Boards of Nursing (NCSBN) has expressed concern about the training and retention of new graduate nurses. If the issue of retention of new graduates is not corrected, the results could have a major impact on the availability of nurses in the United States to meet patient demands for nursing care.

Table 2.2 was retrieved from the NCSBN website and demonstrates the need to create transition-to-practice programs for new graduates (NCSBN, 2015).

TABLE 2.2 THE NEED TO CREATE TRANSITION-TO-PRACTICE PROGRAMS FOR NEW GRADUATES

The Problem	The Impact
New nurses care for sicker patients in increasingly complex health settings.	New nurses report more negative safety practices and errors than experienced nurses.
New nurses feel increased stress levels.	Stress is a risk factor for patient safety and practice errors.
Approximately 25% of new nurses leave a position in their first year of practice.	Increased turnover negatively influences patient safety and health-care outcomes.

©NCSBN, 2015. Excerpted with permission from https://www.ncsbn.org/transition-to-practice.htm

The first year of a new job in any profession is stressful. The transition from nursing student to registered nurse (RN) is one of the most difficult and stressful job transitions (Dyess & Sherman, 2009). The NCSBN has identified the critical elements in Figure 2.2 that can contribute to clinical errors and employee turnover (NCSBN, 2015).

Each new nurse must assimilate into a new work environment. In addition, learning confidence, the application of recently acquired skill, and clinical decision-making is complex. One of the leading nursing experts in transition-to-practice is Patricia Benner, who developed the "Novice to Expert" model of nursing skill development (Benner, 1984). Benner supports situational clinical coaching or guided clinical decision-making to help new graduates transition to practice. She believes coaching is not effective if it is delivered in a non-supportive organizational culture. The environment must welcome new graduates into the organization, be supportive of active learning, and be cognizant of the stress new nurses feel during the first year of nursing (O'Keeffe, 2013).

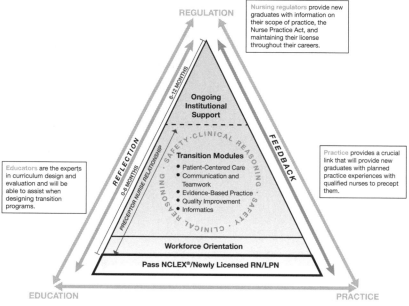

Transition to Practice Model

Figure 2.2 Critical elements that contribute to clinical errors and employee turnover. ©NCSBN, 2015. Excerpted with permission from https://www.ncsbn.org/transition-to-practice.htm.

The NCSBN completed a multi-site study of transition-to-practice, including 105 hospitals in three states, to study the impact of using a model for transition-to-practice. The program was created by the NCSBN and compared transition-to-practice with hospitals that established residency programs with nurses who had limited orientation (Spector et al., 2015). The study involved more than 1,000 newly hired nurses in their first year of work. Survey questions were completed online by participants in four intervals: 1) at baseline, 2) at 6 months, 3) at 9 months, and 4) at 12 months. Post transition, the new registered nurses and the preceptors both completed an assessment of competence (Spector et al., 2015). The study findings concluded that specific outcomes (competence as reported by the new nurses and their linked preceptor; self-reported errors, use of safety practices, work stress, job satisfaction; and hospital data on retention) were significantly better when transition programs had the following characteristics:

- A formalized program that is integrated into the institution, with support from higher administration

- A preceptorship, and the preceptor should be educated for the role

- The program that's 9–12 months in length

- Content that includes patient safety, clinical reasoning, communication and teamwork, patient-centered care, evidence-based practice, quality improvement, and informatics

- Time for new graduates to learn and apply the content and to obtain feedback and share their reflections

- Customization so the new graduates learn specialty content in the areas where they are working

In review of other transition-to-practice studies, the time for new graduate transition-to-practice occurs over an 18-month period (Halfer & Graf, 2006). The most critical time appears to be within the 3 to 12 month time frame. During this time, new nurses struggle with being overwhelmed and feeling that they have too much to do (Halfer & Graf, 2006). At the 12-month mark, nurses who felt satisfied with their job, satisfied with job competencies, experienced professional respect, had easy access to information, and had become part of the team were considered successful (Halfer & Graf, 2006).

The need for transition programs for new graduates has been discussed as early as the 1970s. Marlene Kramer (1974), in her book titled *Reality Shock*, described the transition from an educational setting to the service setting where there is a different set of priorities. Patricia Benner, in her study *From Novice to Expert*, focused on skill acquisition (Benner, 1984). The need for a transition-to-practice has been identified by many organizations, including The Joint Commission, the Institute of Medicine (IOM), and the Carnegie Study of Nursing Education. Each has stated that a residency or transition-to-practice program should be established due to the increasing complexity of healthcare (Spector et al., 2015).

In 2014, data collected in the Spector et al. study indicated that 33% to 48% of hospitals have comprehensive, evidence-based nurse residency programs offered by employers. The programs are more often than not in hospitals with over 250 beds (Spector et al., 2015). In 2009, there were just slightly more than 5,000 hospitals in the United States, according to hospital census data by the Centers for Disease Control. Seventy percent of the hospitals in this study operated fewer than 200 beds (CDC, 2011).

Positive aspects of a residency program for new graduate nurses are the promotion of critical thinking, fostering peer networking and colleague discussions, and support for their professional role transition throughout the first year of practice (Halfer & Graf, 2006). The results from the NCSBN study indicate that a structured transition program decreases errors and negative safety practice in new graduate nurses. In addition, the nurses rated themselves as more competent, had less work-related stress and increased job satisfaction, and were less likely to leave their position during the first year (Spector et al., 2015).

As a profession, the support for transition-to-practice must come from nursing leadership. Nurse leaders in education and clinical practice know the risks and benefits. Nurses are the largest professional group in healthcare. To move the nursing profession to the next level, nurses need to support each other: preceptors and staff, staff with each other, staff and leaders, leaders and educators, and so on. As a new graduate, each nurse must decide how to apply learned practices. Standards are meant to guide appropriate behavior. Having a mentor is key, and these relationships and discussions have a positive influence on the new graduates as they transition into practice (Dyess & Sherman, 2009).

PRACTICE PEARLS

- Nurses must be supportive of their peers.
- Expert nurses must mentor novice nurses.
- Most nurses want to continue learning and apply their recently acquired skills in a supportive environment.
- All nurses want to feel that they are an important part of an effective team.
- Nurses should have opportunities for professional development.

CONCLUSION

Organizational change can't be rushed and always causes some degree of chaos. The healthcare industry is undergoing a wave of unprecedented change. While external forces are driving much of these changes, nurses are central to the new system's success. Thus, this wave provides a positive opportunity, and nurses have a unique set of skills to share in bettering healthcare. Keeping the stressors in perspective will allow an open mind for improvement to evolve. Change takes time, talent, and skill for optimal execution. The next chapter explores nursing as an art versus a science and explains how nursing really is a combination of both.

REFERENCES

Benner, P. (1984). *From novice to expert: Excellence in clinical nursing practice.* Upper Saddle River, NJ: Prentice Hall Health.

Centers for Disease Control and Prevention (CDC). (2011). *Table 116. Hospitals, beds, and occupancy rates, by type of ownership and size of hospital: United States, selected years 1975–2009.* Retrieved from http://www.cdc.gov/nchs/data/hus/2011/116.pdf

Centers for Medicare & Medicaid Services (CMS). (2012). *Frequently asked questions about VBP.* Retrieved from https://www.cms.gov/medicare/quality-initiatives-patient-assessment-instruments/hospital-value-based-purchasing/downloads/fy-2013-program-frequently-asked-questions-about-hospital-vbp-3-9-12.pdf

Centers for Medicare & Medicaid Services (CMS). (2013, November 5). *Quality improvement organization manual.* Retrieved from http://www.cms.gov/Regulations-and-Guidance/Guidance/Manuals/Downloads/qio110c05.pdf

Centers for Medicare & Medicaid Services (CMS). (2014, December 18). *Hospital value-based purchasing.* Retrieved from http://www.cms.gov/Medicare/Quality-Initiatives-Patient-Assessment-Instruments/hospital-value-based-purchasing/index.html

Centers for Medicare & Medicaid Services (CMS). (2015, March 2). *2015 national impact assessment of the Centers for Medicare & Medicaid Services (CMS) quality measures report.* Retrieved from http://www.cms.gov/Medicare/Quality-Initiatives-Patient-Assessment-Instruments/QualityMeasures/Downloads/2015-National-Impact-Assessment-Report.pdf

Dyess, S., & Sherman, R. (2009, September). The first year of practice: New graduate nurses' transition and learning needs. *The Journal of Continuing Education in Nursing, 40*(9), 403–410.

Earl, E. (2015, March 3). *CMS indicates steadily improving quality measures.* Retrieved from http://www.beckershospitalreview.com/quality/cms-indicates-steadily-improving-quality-measures.html

Halfer, D., & Graf, E. (2006, March 24). Graduate nurse perceptions of the work experience. *Nursing Economics, 24*(3), 150–155.

The Joint Commission. (2015, March 6). *Facts about The Joint Commission standards.* Retrieved from http://www.jointcommission.org/facts_about_joint_commission_accreditation_standards/.

Kramer, M. (1974). *Reality shock: Why nurses leave nursing.* St. Louis, MO: Mosby.

Mangan, D. (2014, January 6). Health spending as share of GDP drops for first time since 1997. *CNBC.* Retrieved from http://www.cnbc.com/id/101313516

National Council of State Boards of Nursing (NCSBN). (2015). *Transition to practice*. Retrieved from https://www.ncsbn.org/transition-to-practice.htm

O'Keeffe, M. (2013, April 22). Transition-to-practice programs may contribute to new grad success. *Nurse.com*. Retrieved from https://news.nurse.com/2013/04/22/transition-to-practice-programs-may-contribute-to-new-grad-success/#prettyPhoto

Porter, M. E., & Lee, T. H. (2013, October). The strategy that will fix health care. *Harvard Business Review*. Retrieved from https://hbr.org/2013/10/the-strategy-that-will-fix-health-care&cm_sp=Article

Porter, M. E., & Teisberg, E. (2006). *Redefining health care: Creating value-based competition on results*. Boston, MA: Harvard Business Scoll Press.

Spector, N., Blegen, M., Silvestre, J., Barnsteiner, J., Lynn, M., Ulrich, B., … Alexander, M. (2015, January). Transition to practice study in hospital settings. *Journal of Nursing Regulation, 5*(4), 24–38.

3

NURSING: ART VS. SCIENCE

Suzanne Waddill-Goad, DNP, MBA, RN, CEN
Debra Buck, DNP, MSN, RN

OBJECTIVES

- Consider the characteristics that make nursing an art.

- Consider the characteristics that make nursing a science.

- Consider the characteristics that make nursing both an art and science and their relevance to stress, fatigue, and burnout.

- Learn about case studies showing nursing and the professional stressors in action.

How often do you view a work of art and wonder what inspired the artist to create it? Do you ever wonder what question leads a scientist to pursue knowledge? As a nurse, what inspired you to make your career choice? What is/was the catalyst to pursue nursing as a career? These are all common questions asked on a daily basis.

There are many aspects to choosing a career in nursing that create both intellectual and emotional issues for nurses. How often, when driving home, do you feel the need to call back and check in on a patient? How often can you not let go of the thought that you may have missed something or that there may be one more thing that you forgot to tell the oncoming nurse in the change of shift report? How often do you get easily sidetracked by work-related thoughts and they subsequently impact your life outside of work? For most nurses, these things occur on a daily basis. It is easy to find yourself feeling stressed until you get back to work and make sure the patient is "okay."

All of these unresolved thoughts and associated feelings can lead nurses down the path to burnout. We often take on unnecessary responsibility for patients and others, when so much of it is out of our control. We blame ourselves if a patient's outcome is not favorable. We replay conflict-laden conversations in our heads. Why do we do this? What other profession takes on this type of burden?

Over the years, in personal conversation with friends and peers in the nursing profession, defining what nurses do is somewhat difficult to articulate. Nursing is the scientific basis for the care provided. Nurses can easily recite the normal range of a sodium level or the proper dose of acetaminophen for a 23-pound child. Yet, explaining why a nurse had "a feeling" to double-check a patient because "his or her gut told him or her to" is much more difficult to quantify. Is it instinct? Is it intuition? Is it something that can be learned or was learned in training? Does it come from years of clinical practice?

DEFINING A NURSE

A definition of nursing according to the American Nurses Association (ANA, 2015b, para. 1) is:

> "Nursing is the protection, promotion, and optimization of health and abilities, prevention of illness and injury, alleviation of suffering through the diagnosis and treatment of human response, and advocacy in the care of individuals, families, communities, and populations."

More information can be found at this website: http://www.nursingworld.org/EspeciallyForYou/What-is-Nursing.

The International Council of Nurses (ICN, 2015, para. 1) defines nursing as:

> "Nursing encompasses autonomous and collaborative care of individuals of all ages, families, groups and communities, sick or well and in all settings. Nursing includes the promotion of health, prevention of illness, and the care of ill, disabled and dying people. Advocacy, promotion of a safe environment, research, participation in shaping health policy and in patient and health systems management, and education are also key nursing roles."

More information can be found at this website: http://www.icn.ch/who-we-are/icn-definition-of-nursing/.

According to the National Council of State Boards of Nursing (NCSBN, 2015), a nurse is:

> "An individual who has graduated from a state-approved school of nursing, passed the NCLEX-RN examination,

and is licensed by a state board of nursing to provide patient care."

More information can be found at this website: https://www.ncsbn.org/nursing-terms.htm.

Given the multiple and differing definitions of nursing, it is not difficult to understand why nurses have problems describing exactly what they do and why they do it. A question often asked, that further adds to the confusion by both those in and out of the profession, is, "What is nursing: an art or science?"

PRACTICE PEARLS

- Trust your "gut" or intuition.
- If something doesn't "feel" right, it probably isn't.
- Use the available evidence—it can make or break your practice.

NURSING AS AN ART

Chinn (1994) described art as not something that stands in opposition to science but as a part of all human experience. Art can express a feeling or what words usually fail to express. Art can bring a comprehensive experience to human consciousness if people are aware.

Artistic characteristics of nursing include:

- Creativity
- Intuition
- Insight

- Passion

- Collaboration

Lindeman (1999), in an editorial, summarized previous work by researchers Dock and Stewart from the 1920s about the art of nursing. Lindeman described how nursing would be lost, and possibly dangerous, without being guided by science. However, no amount of knowledge will ever make up for the lack of skills that constitute the art of nursing and it is not something that can be formalized. As with any form of art, it reflects perceptions from the viewer and the art or artist who is performing.

Florence Nightingale stated:

> "Nursing is an art; and if it is made to be an art, it requires
> as exclusive a devotion, as hard a preparation, as any painter's
> or sculptor's work; for what is having to do with dead canvas
> or cold marble, compared with having to do with the living
> body—the temple of God's spirit? It is one of the fine arts;
> I had almost said the finest of fine arts." (Dossey, 1999, p. 7;
> finestquotes.com, n.d.)

Finfgeld-Connett (2008), in her concept synthesis of the art of nursing, referenced relationship-centered practice and the artistic characteristics present in nursing. The artistic characteristics include kindness, compassion, healing touch, humor, and thoughtful doing. For nurses to provide this type of approach to patient care, they must be at their best. Developing a calm demeanor, a sense of confidence with a peaceful spirit, and high regard for what they do is essential. This type of practice leaves little room for those who are stressed, fatigued, and burned out. Patient interaction encompasses all of these characteristics and can be explained through practice examples. A series of examples, listed as cases, are presented throughout this chapter to illustrate nursing art versus science. In each of the cases, consider if what is described was learned behavior for the nurses to act as they did. Or was it simple human kindness? How do we explain the "art of nursing"?

CASE EXAMPLES: NURSING AS AN ART

Case 1: A 2-year-old had been a frequent patient in the intensive care unit. She had undergone multiple shunt revisions for hydrocephalus. The multiple revisions left a great deal of scar tissue along with a complication during the last revision. Both left her gravely ill and on a ventilator to assist her breathing; she was unresponsive to stimuli. One of the night shift nurses who worked in the unit read to her every night and made sure that she had her own pajamas and her favorite stuffed animal with her. A bond had formed between the nurse and child. All of the staff knew the child would not survive. The night that she died, the nurse was on duty. She refused to let the child be taken to the morgue on the morgue cart. She wrapped her in her favorite blanket and carried her down the back steps to the morgue.

Case 2: A young woman was in an auto accident, sustaining a severe head injury. She spent several weeks in the intensive care unit (ICU). A request was made to her family to bring in familiar items that she enjoyed, along with music. Her husband was a youth pastor and had a beautiful voice. Each day, he would come to her room and sing to her. Several of the staff, if time permitted, would join him and sing all of her favorite hymns. Often, other patients' family members would stand outside the door to hear the music. Other patients in the ICU would comment on how much they enjoyed the music. The patient went to rehabilitation for her injuries and made a marvelous recovery. After her discharge home, she commented to her husband that she remembered hearing choir music almost every day she was in the hospital.

Case 3: A patient with Guillain-Barre syndrome spent several weeks in the hospital. He was an avid football fan and loved to watch the games on Sunday. Several of the nurses cared for him over the time he was hospitalized. On one of the Sundays, he thought the staff should all be involved in a football pool on the games for the day. The nurses who were on duty that day gladly granted his request. After his recovery was complete, he sent a thank-you note to the staff commenting on how that day made him feel "normal" again.

Case 4: On a busy night in the emergency department (ED), a radio call went out for a multiple fatality motor vehicle collision. One of the emergency medical service (EMS) crews who responded to the scene came into the ED on a separate call later in the evening. One of the EMS crew members was found in the utility room crying about the earlier call. Two little boys, brothers, had been killed in the accident. A beautiful baby girl was in the department with colic. She had settled down and was "a happy baby" waiting for discharge. One of the nurses talked with her parents and asked to "borrow" her for a few minutes. The nurse took the baby, walked over to the EMS crew member in the utility room, and placed the baby in his arms. She smiled and cooed at him. The nurse looked at the EMS crew member and made a simple statement, "Life goes on."

Case 5: A nurse was passing medications late in the evening. She entered a patient room to give the medications. The patient was in pain due to a kidney stone and had recently received a pain medication dosage to attempt to alleviate some of the pain. The nurse was busy and running behind. The patient made a simple request. "Can you please just sit and talk with me for a minute?" The nurse began to think of all she had to do before the end of her shift. However, she made the decision to sit with the patient. They had a wonderful conversation. During that time, the patient relaxed, and before the nurse left the room, he dozed off.

Each of these cases describes how a nurse's thoughts and subsequent behaviors were able to immensely comfort and influence others in a time of need. Being mindful, present, and not distracted—taking the time to notice another's distress—made all the difference to each of these patients. This "presence" requires nurses to skillfully cultivate a positive relationship with both stressors and stress.

PRACTICE PEARLS

- Listen to your patients.
- Listen to the patient's parents and/or caregivers.
- Consider taking the time you need to encompass the art of nursing into your daily work representing the science of nursing. It will improve your practice.
- Think about how your stress impacts your work and the patients or others you care for in your work environment.
- When you're feeling stressed, take a moment to think about the experience you are having and the experience you would like to be having. How big is the gap?

THE INTUITIVE PART OF NURSING

Finfgeld-Connett (2008) references the terms *empirical* and *metaphysical* knowledge in relation to the art of nursing. *Metaphysical* addresses characteristics that are not always apparent yet are intuitive to nursing practice. It is an important portion of nursing, and it relies on the nurse being in tune with the patient, peers, and most importantly, with himself or herself.

No one patient is the same as the next. Even two patients' diagnoses may be the same, yet every other clinical and behavioral characteristic they exhibit are different. This generally produces a wide variety of outcomes.

Nurses need to be able to recognize and acknowledge these differences to better care for each individual patient. Through the acknowledgment of these differences, a nurse is better able to help patients to achieve their optimal levels of health. Caring for each patient individually requires careful thought and calculated risk-taking to address differences to meet each patient's needs. An example is presented in the following case.

Case 6: A new graduate nurse was working on a surgical floor. Due to the fact that she was the newest nurse in the department, she was assigned a patient that the rest of the staff on her shift felt was "difficult" and they did not want to care for. The new nurse entered the patient's room and immediately encountered a very angry woman who suddenly began to cry. The nurse sat with her and asked her why she was angry. The patient shared with the nurse that she was the first one to acknowledge that she was angry and began to share the story of her illness along with her fears. The nurse and the patient developed a bond that lasted through each of her admissions and, subsequently, her death.

The nurse in this case was in tune with her own feelings and chose not to enter the patient's room with a preconceived idea secondary to her peers' perceptions of the situation. She took a risk by asking the patient a difficult question. The patient could have chosen not to share her feelings with the nurse and to take her anger out on the new nurse. By taking this risk, the new nurse helped to care for this patient by acknowledging her anger and removing it as a barrier.

Johnson (1994) reviewed all of the available literature relevant to the art of nursing and came up with the following summary. There are five distinct concepts that help to identify nursing as an art. These five concepts can be found in each of the cases presented and include:

- Embracing the meaning in patient encounters

- Establishing a connection with the patient

- Skillfully performing nursing activities

- Developing a course of action to care for patients

- Conducting your own practice of nursing morally

Blondeau (2002) looked at nursing as a practical art and emphasized the concept of artistic knowledge in nursing through Adler's (1978) definition. Adler defined artistic knowledge as "making anything" and mentions that productive ideas are not enough to create an end product. Making things requires the knowledge and skill to take raw materials and create something more. If there is no end product then there is no realization of the idea, and it cannot be expressed.

Adler's (1978) definition of artistic knowledge can be applied to the practice of nursing. The definition can best be described by applying it to a patient interaction:

A patient presents with a set of symptoms that they have developed. The patient is otherwise healthy and takes no medication. A nurse performs an initial assessment of the patient and relays the information to the medical provider. The medical provider assesses the symptoms (raw materials), orders testing and, based on the findings (raw materials), prescribes a course of treatment (raw materials). The nurse carries out the orders and educates (something created from raw materials) the patient on the prescribed course of treatment. The patient acknowledges the treatment plan and schedules a follow-up appointment. Upon return for the follow-up appointment, the patient's symptoms have been alleviated and he has returned to a state of health (something created).

Chinn (1994) declared the art of nursing as the art/act of the experience in the moment. It is the direct apprehension of a situation, the intuitive and embodied knowing, that arises from the practice/praxis of nursing. Through this definition, the science of nursing can be interpreted to coincide with the art. What makes a nurse return to a room to check on a patient he or she just left? How does a nurse know what to do in a crisis with a patient he or she has never met? When a disaster strikes, why is it the nurse who is relied on to handle the situation?

PRACTICE PEARLS

- Every patient has a story to tell—listen.
- Be creative in your practice of nursing.
- To be at your best, take time for the "three R's": rest, recover, and refuel.

NURSING AS A SCIENCE

To define the science of nursing, differences must be examined within science itself. In 1966, Hemple distinguished between natural and social sciences. Natural sciences include physics, chemistry, and biology and incorporate other areas such as anatomy and physiology. The social sciences, according to Hemple (1966), may include sociology, political science, anthropology, and economics.

Hemple (1966) went on to discuss that science is empirical and non-empirical. Empirical science attempts to describe, explain, and predict what occurs in the world we live in. Much of what is done in nursing is non-empirical and falls under the category of social science. Nurses build a practice from the empirical science, as it provides the basis for the individualized care each patient receives.

Scientific characteristics of nursing include:

- Deduction

- Fact finding

- Observation

- Testing and proving/disproving theories

- Collaborating

Manhart-Barrett (2002) defined nursing as a basic science; it is the application of the scientific art of using knowledge to practice nursing. Others define science in a slightly different way as being a collective body of knowledge comprised of applied research along with testing theories. Research findings and the development of theories can be applied to generally any area and certainly to a specific discipline such as nursing.

Parse et al. (2000) developed a definition of nursing science that is continually evolving. They define nursing science as a basic science. It encompasses substantive knowledge of the human-universe-health process while being discipline-based.

These definitions lead to a question of significance. Cody (as cited in Daly et al., 1997) put forth a warning—the difficulty that nursing has as a profession with articulating what it does, and its unique nature within healthcare, have placed nursing at risk. Similarly, Nagle (1999) stated that nursing can be a matter of distinction or extinction. These views, albeit close to two decades old, bear a great deal of truth in nursing today.

For experienced nurses, the ability to articulate the nursing process is defined by distinct steps. It begins with the assessment of a patient. The findings based on the assessment lead a nurse to plan interventions for the patient, with the patient. Those interventions are then implemented. After the interventions are implemented, at defined intervals, nurses reassess the effectiveness of the interventions. If the interventions are effective, the same course is followed. If the interventions are not effective, the entire process begins again—assessment of the patient, creating a care plan, implementation of clinical and non-clinical interventions, and evaluation of the process.

In recent times, this process has been expanded to include other elements such as nursing diagnosis and outcomes (ANA, 2015b). More information about the nursing process can be found here: http://www. nursingworld.org/EspeciallyForYou/What-is-Nursing/Tools-You-Need/ Thenursingprocess.html.

There are some nurses in the profession who may question if this portion of the science of nursing has been replaced with clinical pathways and prompts in the electronic health or medical record that only require the click of a radio button. Or what about smart pumps that don't require a nurse to calculate the correct drip rate of a medication? Listening to a patient's apical pulse to count a heart rate is often done via a cardiac monitor. The cardiac monitor may not even be in the same room as the patient. The individual trained to surveil the monitor(s) is generally not a nurse. Automatic blood pressure cuffs are relied upon to take an accurate blood pressure. Pulse oximeters measure oxygen saturation, and other technologic advances measure key vital signs; today's nurse just has to look at the readout on a machine. However, interpretation—which takes into account all that a nurse sees with the patient—cannot be accomplished by machinery. Does this advancement of technology take away from the science in nursing practice? Are today's nurses too dependent on equipment when they used to be dually dependent on assessment skills and knowledge? Critical thinking and reasoning cannot be replaced by technology.

Case 7: A recent anecdotal example of this issue occurred when an ED physician responded to an in-house incident in which a patient's condition was rapidly declining. The physician requested a current blood pressure on the patient and then watched as the nursing staff repeatedly pushed the button on the automatic blood pressure cuff in the attempt to get a blood pressure. The physician, in a moment of frustration, asked if anyone knew how to take a manual blood pressure.

A recent article written by Feliciano (2014) on Nursetogether.com referenced a statement made by Dr. Rosalind Picard, a Massachusetts Institute of Technology professor who feels that robots should be made available to physicians and nurses to enhance the delivery of care. Feliciano (2014) noted efforts currently underway that could potentially lead to robots replacing nurses. Is that even possible? Have nurses become so dependent on technology that they could be replaced? Have nurses drifted away from the science that is the foundation for nursing practice?

Manhart-Barrett (2002) referenced previous work by other researchers in the 1990s who defined the science of nursing as a scholarly discipline, overlapping with other disciplines, all the while encompassing all that nurses do. Nursing is more than just providing care. Nursing science is theory- and research-based, as it requires specialized knowledge and utilizes methods other than those that are solely based in nursing science. However, nursing science is the core or essence of the discipline.

Idczak (2007) posited that the science of nursing finds its base in the acquisition of skills and knowledge that occurs throughout the nursing curriculum. The concept of *relatedness backward* describes how the skills are acquired in nursing. In this concept, the nurse acquires knowledge through looking back at a process and methodically scrutinizing the process to determine two things: what could have been done better and what worked well for the patient. An example of this process, which is extreme yet defines it well, is presented in the following case.

Case 8: A patient is to be transferred from the emergency department (ED) to the critical care unit (CCU) following the application of an external pacemaker for a heart block. Cardiac rhythm capture has been maintained, and the patient is delivered to the CCU. During the admission process, the patient is switched to the equipment that is present in the CCU. Cardiac rhythm capture was lost during the exchange, and the patient did not survive. A root cause analysis (RCA) was conducted to determine the cause of the incident. All staff involved in the case were brought together in an attempt to gather information and understand what went wrong. This RCA process was meant to ensure this type of incident would not occur again. The nurses involved painstakingly reviewed every aspect of the case, including their care from the nursing perspective, and made recommendations to prevent any future instances.

While this case is extreme, each nurse learned from the incident, and most likely, it will forever affect their practice.

CONCLUSION

There is no black-and-white answer to the question, is nursing an art or a science? All nurses, regardless of where they are in their career path, what degree or degrees they hold, and what department or setting they work in, could give you a definition and multiple examples to support art or science, or both.

Nurses must be mindful to be at their best in caring for others. Mind "stress" only exists in what has happened in the past and what might come in the future—not generally in the present. Emergent circumstances may dictate stress and appropriate action in the present. Thus, nurses need to be "mentally fit" as well as physically able to perform.

As technology continues to become more of a part of the practice of nursing, pieces of both the art and science will be replaced. Yet, as nursing research continues to evolve, clinical guidelines become standard, and evidence-based practices are implemented, new nursing science will become prevalent. Science can never replace the art that fills an amazingly diverse profession. If one were to ask any patient who has been afraid before a procedure and a nurse held the patient's hand and provided comfort, he or she will tell you just how special the nurse was. If one were to talk to a family who tragically lost a loved one, most likely they would be able to describe how compassionate the nurse was that helped them through the paperwork as an expert guide. Gather a group of nurses together and they will share how a peer comforted them after a terrible shift.

If one were to ask a group of nurses to describe how they knew to re-check a patient, they will respond, "I just knew." The same group of nurses could also describe the many times they called back to check on a patient after the shift ended. It might even have been in the middle of the night. When asked if there is another profession most nurses would choose, nurses emphatically state that there is nothing that they would rather do.

To be a dedicated artist requires commitment, sacrifice, talent, and a desire to create something beautiful, often out of something that others will never see the beauty in. They make many sacrifices. Nurses work odd hours, off shifts, and holidays. They frequently miss family gatherings and milestones in their children's lives. They sleep through a concert because they have been up for 36 hours. Christmas is often moved to another day on the calendar because it is their holiday to work. Nurses often leave their shift hungry, exhausted, and barely able to think about what has to be done at home or in other aspects of their lives.

Nurses witness more horror in a single day than most other professions in a lifetime. A distraught mother hands a nurse her lifeless child and expects the nurse to save her. A husband loses his wife of 60 years and cries on the nurse's shoulder; all the while, the nurse understands that it won't be long before he joins her.

Nurses are like a piece of marble, and the experiences are the hammer and chisel in the hands of the sculptor. Each patient cared for, each interaction with peers, each life experience slowly chips away, revealing more and more of the beauty beneath the surface. That beauty comes through in the way the nurse interacts with patients, peers, family, friends, and complete strangers. It is the beauty that shines in the darkest moments. The moments might include a nurse sitting with a family that tragically lost their 17-year-old son in an auto accident or the 88-year-old man whose wife passed away after 70 years of marriage. It is there when a physician delivers difficult news to a patient and the nurse is left at the bedside to "pick up the pieces" and help a patient and family comprehend what they have just been told. The beauty also shines through when a nurse sees a patient walk for the first time after a major injury or hands a baby to a new parent.

Can nursing be quantified? Is it possible based on the components that are easy to define? And others that are fleeting? Is it an art or a science? It might just be for each individual to decide.

In the next chapter, you will learn about nursing leadership. Nursing leadership is often intertwined with diverse stressors; nurse leaders regularly navigate among a multitude of stressful conditions in their daily work. These conditions often produce immense stress, leading to fatigue and burnout.

REFERENCES

Adler, M. (1978a). *Art and prudence*. New York, NY: Arno Press.

American Nurses Association (ANA). (2015a). *What is nursing?* Retrieved from http://www.nursingworld.org/EspeciallyForYou/What-is-Nursing

American Nurses Association (ANA). (2015b). *The nursing process*. Retrieved from http://www.nursingworld.org/EspeciallyForYou/What-is-Nursing/Tools-You-Need/Thenursingprocess.html

Blondeau, D. (2002). Nursing art as a practical art: The necessary relationship between nursing art and nursing ethics. *Nursing Philosophy, 3*(3), 252–259. doi: 10.1046/j.1466-769X.2002.00095.x

Chinn, P. (1994). Arts and aesthetics in nursing. *Advances in Nursing Science, 17*(1).

Daly, J., Mitchell, G., Toikkanen, T., Millar, B., Zanotti, R., & Takahashi, T. (1997). What is nursing science? An international dialogue. *Nursing Science Quarterly, 10,* 10–13.

Dossey, B. (1999). A Nightingale legacy: The art of nursing. *Creative Nursing, 5*(3), 7–9.

Feliciano, C. (2014, February 14). Robot replacing nurses: Is it really that far-fetched? *Nursetogether.com.* Retrieved from http://www.nursetogether.com/robot-replacing-nurses-is-it-really-that-f

Finestquotes.com. (n.d.). Florence Nightingale quotes. Retrieved from http://www.finestquotes.com/author_quotes-author-florence%20nightingale-page-0.htm

Finfgeld-Connett, D. (2008). Concept synthesis of the art of nursing. *Journal of Advanced Nursing, 62*(3), 381–388. doi: 10.1111/j.1365-2648.2008.04601.x

Hemple, C. (1966). *Philosophy of natural science*. Upper Saddle River, NJ: Prentice-Hall.

Idczak, S. E. (2007). I am a nurse: Nursing students learn the art and science of nursing. *Nursing Education Perspectives, 28*(2), 66–71.

International Council of Nurses (ICN). (2015). *Definition of nursing*. Retrieved from http://www.icn.ch/who-we-are/icn-definition-of-nursing/

Johnson, J. (1994). A dialectical examination of nursing art. *Advances in Nursing Science, 17*(1), 1–14.

Lindeman, C. (1999). From the guest editor: The art of nursing. *Creative Nursing, 5*(3), 3–4.

Manhart-Barrett, E. (2002). What is nursing science? *Nursing Science Quarterly, 15*(1), 51–60.

Nagle, L. (1999). A matter of extinction or distinction. *Western Journal of Nursing Research, 21*(1), 71–82. doi:10.1177/01939459922043712

National Council of State Boards of Nursing (NCSBN). (2015). *Definition of nursing terms.* Retrieved from https://www.ncsbn.org/nursing-terms.htm

Parse, R., Barrett, E., Bourgeois, M., Dee, V., Eagen, E., & Germain, C. (2000). Nursing theory guided practice: A definition. *Nursing Science Quarterly, 13,* 177.

4

THE IMPACT OF NURSING LEADERSHIP

Suzanne Waddill-Goad, DNP, MBA, RN, CEN
Debra Buck, DNP, MSN, RN

OBJECTIVES

- Explore the idea of leadership.
- Consider the characteristics that make a good leader.
- Consider how good leadership mitigates stress.
- Learn techniques for lowering stress in a leadership position.

There is a great debate taking place in nearly every work setting about leadership. Are great leaders born or developed over time? Can leaders be shaped and created, or is leadership an instinct? Further discussion begs the question, is there a difference between leadership and management?

What we do know is that leadership matters. It is perhaps the single most important element in any successful business enterprise (Mills, 2005). Leaders must not be afraid to take risks. Not everyone who either chooses or ends up in a leadership role is meant to be a leader. The impact a nurse leader can make—good or bad—is critical to the development of healthy workplace culture, the resulting work environment, and subsequent organizational performance. All nurses should be viewed as leaders due to their ability to influence others' decision-making.

Leaders create structure through social interaction (Marion & Uhl-Bien, 2001). Noudelman (2015) diagnosed today's organizations as suffering from a recognition problem; they can't distinguish good leaders from bad ones. He describes weak leaders as follows (Noudelman, 2015):

- Their team routinely suffers from burnout.
- They lack emotional intelligence.
- They don't provide adequate direction.
- They find blame in everyone but themselves.
- They don't provide honest feedback.
- They are blind to the current situation.
- They are self-serving.

Unfortunately, Noudelman's description describes some leaders of today in nursing and healthcare. Their leadership behavior negatively influences the work environment. Stress, fatigue, and burnout among the workforce are all evident in these types of work cultures. A number of years ago, a training video depicting the culture of Southwest Airlines was developed to show the value of loyalty between a company and its employees; it described how to utilize trust to increase employee morale, develop superior customer service, and impact the company bottom line. Incidentally, Southwest Airlines has sustained positive financial performance in the difficult aviation industry where most all of its competitors have struggled.

A similar comparison can be made with healthcare leadership. It is so simple—the "golden rule" (treat others as you would like to be treated) goes a long way, and a servant leadership type attitude should be a foundational element for leaders in healthcare, and especially in nursing. In addition, being nice and treating others with respect is just basic human kindness.

Robert K. Greenleaf coined the term *servant leadership* and first published his thoughts in an essay in the 1970s (Greenleaf Center for Servant Leadership, n.d., p. 3). Greenleaf describes *servant leadership* as:

> "The servant-leader is servant first... It begins with the natural feeling that one wants to serve, to serve first. Then conscious choice brings one to aspire to lead. That person is sharply different from one who is leader first, perhaps because of the need to assuage an unusual power drive or to acquire material possessions."

A servant-leader focuses primarily on the growth and well-being of people and the communities to which they belong.

WHAT IS LEADERSHIP?

A single definition of leadership in the literature is elusive. Most descriptions of leaders are based on the context or the situation. A search of the nursing-specific literature revealed a multitude of examples offering differing singular definitions. Perhaps Noudelman's (2015) definition could be used in reverse to describe good leadership. If so, it would look like this:

- Their team is considered a dream team of leaders.

- They exhibit emotional intelligence.

- Their expectations are clear, and they are decisive when necessary.

- They insist on a "no-blame culture."

- They provide honest and candid feedback.

- They are aware of the current state of organizational affairs based on accurate data.

- They exude an attitude of service.

Working for that type of leader sounds great, right? It also fits with what healthcare needs most to move forward in the whirlwind of current change.

PRACTICE PEARL

"Do not follow where the path may lead. Go instead where there is no path and leave a trail." —Anonymous

A memorable leader in history, Eleanor Roosevelt, was noted for her informal style. Her thoughts about leadership could be used today as guiding principles for nursing and healthcare:

- "You can often change your circumstances by changing your attitude; do one thing every day that scares you." This encourages leaders to reflect on their contribution and be willing to question the status quo and take risks.

- "Do what you feel in your heart to be right for you as you will be criticized anyway." This encourages leaders to follow their intuition and always do what is right no matter what the consequences.

- "To handle yourself, use your head; to handle others, use your heart." This encourages leaders to be thoughtful and caring when taking risks and driving change.

More pithy quotes from Eleanor Roosevelt can be found at https://www.goodreads.com/author/quotes/44566.Eleanor_Roosevelt.

Leadership can come from any position in nursing: the staff nurse, charge nurse, nursing supervisors, nursing educators, nurse manager and directors, as well as nurses in formal executive leadership roles (such as vice presidents and chiefs). Healthcare needs nursing leadership at all levels. One person can make a positive or negative difference from his or her contribution, and this includes behavior as well as actions. Think about Florence Nightingale, Mother Teresa, Clara Barton, and Dorothea Dix (Online BSN, 2009). Which type of nurse are you? Are you a positive or a negative influence?

One of the greatest things leaders can do is be creative in their approach to problem-solving. Much of what used to work in nursing and healthcare is no longer relevant. Nikravan (2012) described exceptional leaders as those who help employees work through times of change by communicating extensively. Explaining the need for change and ensuring everyone understands the change increases the odds that the change will be successful.

PRACTICE PEARLS

- Leadership can come from any organizational position (informal versus formal).
- Be a positive leadership influence on others—attitude is everything.
- Nursing is a service profession—be a good example to others.

THE LEADERSHIP-STRESS CONNECTION

Carlson (2009) described the chaos-filled healthcare environment as one with a dizzying pace of change, with leaders showing weariness to continue, thus creating various degrees of satisfaction, too much positional turnover, health-related symptoms of stress, and a tendency to want to quit. Later, Waddill-Goad (2013) outlined stress as a concern in healthcare, specifically with executive nurses, relative to multiple perspectives as a negatively contributing factor with strong organizational impact. Stress is known to lead to higher healthcare costs, inefficiency, staff turnover, increased sickness, and absenteeism in the workplace. These effects have been noted by the many diverse industries that have studied the effects of stress.

Shirey (2006) suggested stress is a negative factor in healthcare and nursing in a study over nearly two decades. Stress was shown to decrease the quality and the quantity of care, as well as job satisfaction.

In a landmark leadership study, also over a 20-year period, Lieberson and O'Connor (1972) looked at the link between leadership and corporate and environmental factors influencing organizational performance in 167 public companies. Their findings suggest that leaders are restricted in their ability to influence results due to the internal structure of an organization and its culture by blocked communication, factional conflict, and abortive bureaucracy. These results beg the question, "If there was more effective communication, less conflict, and less bureaucracy in the healthcare work environment, would nurses (as well as others) be less stressed, and would the organization achieve better results?"

Guyton (2012) reviewed a number of principles for successful nursing leadership. The first principle is a commitment to excellence. This aptly applies to all nurses. Everything related to nursing should meet a standard of excellence; a nurse's span of influence includes everything from caring for a patient to promoting the nursing profession in a positive manner.

Another of Guyton's principles (2012) is to measure the things that are important. Currently, two of nursing's most important regulatory metrics are patient experience and patient outcomes. In the measurement of patient satisfaction or experience, the connection between nurse satisfaction and patient satisfaction is often overlooked. Nauert (n.d.) pointed out there is a direct correlation between customer satisfaction and employee satisfaction; the improvement is almost two-fold when employees have a high level of job satisfaction. In practice, this also seems to correlate. Happy employees lead to happier customers.

In addition to the metrics of patient experience and outcomes, growth and finance cannot be neglected (Guyton, 2012). Nurse leaders need to be good role models with expert communication, planning, and finance skills. Information in the new age of healthcare needs to be shared, and organizations must be transparent. As previously described, employee engagement is necessary for the most successful outcomes in both business and service. Engaging healthcare employees is perhaps more necessary now than ever before with the new pay-for-performance compensable metrics.

Guyton's (2012) principle, building a culture around service, is explained well by a servant leadership attitude. Nurse leaders have an opportunity to serve many others by the decisions they make: medical care providers, patients, nurses, and other clinicians. Their decisions can result in the design of good systems, outcomes, and culture—or just the opposite. A culture in which customers and employees both feel valued is ideal and easily achievable in healthcare. In addition, one of the hallmark metrics of good leadership is low turnover; turnover is often solely caused from poor relationships between the involved parties.

Nothing causes more stress and frustration for leaders than vacancies with more work to be done than can be accomplished. Why do most people change jobs? The research suggests it is due to a less than optimal relationship with their direct supervisor. This also seems to be so simple—it is everyone's professional responsibility to create good relationships and a good work environment. When successful, other problems often take care of themselves. Most measurable results in healthcare—employee, provider, and patient satisfaction or experiences, as well as financial and quality performance—are tightly intertwined with good relationship-building, efficient communication, and a healthy work environment.

BEING A GOOD LEADER

Building new leader programs or succession planning is vital for any organization, regardless of size. In smaller organizations, it is perhaps even more important. The fourth principle Guyton (2012) addressed was creating and developing leaders. A structured system of leadership succession is important for current and future leaders. Expectations are more clearly outlined, the desired characteristics and results are known, and organizations can create an effective leadership pipeline. Identifying internal and external talent is critical for optimal organizational skill planning. Frequently, internal informal leaders have a tremendous amount of influence and organizational knowledge. Commonly, what is needed is a formal system to hone their rudimentary leadership skills.

Guyton's (2012) additional and cited as vitally important principles are communication, accountability, reward, and recognition. Accountability begins with communicating clear expectations. Holding individuals accountable for their actions is a leadership skill that can be problematic to master; conversations about performance are often difficult, and leaders must develop a tolerance for conflict. Many aspects of accountability are dependent on organizational policy and procedures. A single standard of leader communication, consistency, and follow-through is crucial.

Inconsistencies in communication cause confusion, which in turn causes stress and affects morale. Take caution to prevent information overload. Consider multiple methods of communication to reach all intended parties. This includes written communications such as memos, email, etc. Other verbal communication channels such as huddles, informal hallway conversations, and short meetings can be used to reinforce written communiqués or for conversation and/or clarity. All communication strategies must embrace honesty, be timely and simple to reach, and be understood by a diverse audience.

Success needs to be celebrated. Leaders and organizations who value employee contributions will reap the rewards. Giving credit where it's due and praising performance can go a long way. This is particularly important when individuals, groups, departments, and organizations are challenged. As leaders, it is easy to move on to the next thing or priority. However, it is often the small things that make a difference in employee satisfaction. A simple hello, taking time to ask about how someone is doing, and being visible all yield positive rewards for leaders and staff.

Reward and recognition are key strategies to making people feel valued. Taking the time to acknowledge employees for their professional contribution and personal accomplishments carries a tremendous amount of weight. All too regularly, it is easy to focus on what is not going right versus what is. Nurses are trained to look for what is wrong. Decisions are made by a process of elimination. We need to change the focus to looking for what is working and what can be improved. This change in thinking might change the perception of what is causing stress, fatigue, and burnout due to "uncontrollable" external forces.

PRACTICE PEARLS

- Strive for effective communication to build solid relationships. Only engage in healthy conflict and respectful debates. Less conflict means less stress.
- Pay attention to what is being measured in your work environment. What is your involvement and contribution?
- Learn about leadership and work to eliminate bureaucracy.
- Recognize a job well done and be accountable.

Strategies to combat stress must be integrated into nursing and healthcare systems. Grossman and Valiga (2009) describe four "Ts" of leadership: truth, trust, teamwork, and training. Each is easy to implement into existing systems of leadership and communication.

The first is truth—leaders must be truthful even when the news is not good. Trust is built by being truthful. Effective relationships require truth and trust. Teamwork is the third "T" and relies on a foundation built by truth and trust. The fourth "T" is training; it is essential to stay current with evidence-based industry practices.

According to Dudiy (2005), these simple guidelines facilitate better teamwork and team building:

- Goals should be clear, understood, and accepted by the team members.

- Team clarity is essential, and roles must be defined and responsibilities assigned.

- Each team member must make a valuable contribution (in order to be heard).

PRACTICE PEARLS

- Team goals, roles, and guidelines must be clear.
- All team members must be invested in the outcome.
- Communication must flow freely and be truthful.

STRUCTURE/PROCESS/ OUTCOME IN SYSTEMS

The design of an organizational structure is critical because it drives the subsequent work processes. Donabedian (1980) noted the structure/process/outcome connection in relation to quality. It also fittingly applies to business. Structure drives processes, which subsequently drive outcomes (good or bad) in a generally predictable fashion. The good largely drives good outcomes and the poor largely drives poor outcomes. Much of what transpires in healthcare is not all that unpredictable.

There are patterns of predicting outcomes if you look at data. Healthcare has enormous amounts of data in current electronic systems. However, turning the data from often disparate systems into useful information has been historically challenging. Data-driven decision-making has also not been the consistent norm among nursing leaders. This is changing due to the number of required quality indicators, publicly reported data, and focus on the clinical outcomes' connection to reimbursement or payment.

Design review can begin either at the top or at the base of an organizational structure. From the top, it might include analysis of the number of leadership roles, direct reports, span of control, and associated departmental fit with divisional responsibility. From the base, it may include analysis of skill mix, staffing patterns and plans, models of care delivery, and customer type and demand.

Each of the design elements drives work process. *Work process* consists of a number of steps that may be sequenced, dependent on previous results or independent of either. In recent years, a number of healthcare organizations have embarked on journeys to incorporate Lean or Six Sigma principles into their operations. Both strategies have the ability to decrease variation, decrease defects, and improve overall cost and quality. Each begins with a standard approach to problem-solving with a review of process steps and associated outcomes. Once the process (supported by data) is understood, changes can be recommended.

Healthcare is the most complex knowledge-driven industry in the world and represents one of the most important economic challenges in recent history (Glaser & Hess, 2011). Cox (2002) posited that you can transform something important into something urgent if you wait long enough. Healthcare seems to have been a "neglected" system, allowed to evolve on its own. Common nursing procedures or business as usual has habitually layered new forms, techniques, and plans with little regard for past process analysis. The absence of innovation, forward-thinking leadership, and efficient system management has resulted in challenges of process, access, equity, and quality.

A sense of urgency needs to become the new norm; inaction will be even more costly. Nursing is constantly changing, so nurses cannot sit idly by and do nothing. Nurse leaders need to set the tone to embrace change. Nurses also need to embrace change. Key traits for all of today's nurses should include competency in system design, planning, explanation, and project implementation.

PRACTICE PEARLS

- Does the organizational design support patient-care needs? Are the right people doing the right work?
- Does the department have efficient work processes? Does the work environment support good work flow (traffic patterns, location of equipment and supply, etc.)?
- Is leadership supportive of change related to improvement?

LEADERSHIP STRATEGIES TO MITIGATE STRESS

Interpersonal challenges can be one of the most concerning issues facing nurse leaders. Conflict causes a host of problems within organizations. Nurse leaders must become stress-tolerant to succeed in their assigned roles. They are often balancing priorities from a variety of sources: internal and external customer demands, financial pressures, labor shortages, as well as many others. Confidentiality is often required, and the inability to share information may potentiate feelings of stress. This requires nurse leaders to balance professionalism with honesty and integrity.

Nurse leaders can suitably apply the nursing process method of problem-solving to organizational maladies. Objectivity is key, and they must accurately assess the data in challenging situations as the first step. They must then analyze the available information, using their ability to ascertain whether additional material is required. They should only draw conclusions after careful assessment and analysis of the evidence and devise plans for a course of action, leaving time for appropriate pauses with evaluation. Timing might be everything. Rarely do others perceive organizational emergencies as true emergencies. Problems in general do not develop overnight and should not be solved in a thoughtless and/or reckless manner due to panic.

Thoughtful leaders take time to make decisions, take time for themselves, and make time for others. Sometimes taking time is the best strategy to decrease stress, fatigue, and the potential for burnout. The amount of time is relative; it might be a short break, a real vacation, or time in between jobs.

A great deal of information is currently found in the literature about mindfulness. *Mindfulness* is simply defined as being aware and present. Awareness includes feelings, thoughts, and attention focused on the present moment. Rarely do we take time to stop "doing" and just "be."

Future success should not be associated with busyness. Multitasking is a misnomer. When you are multitasking, you are not present in either task.

Mindful individuals notice those who are not present. A lack of presence or not being in the moment and appearing disrespectful may signal trouble for leaders.

Engaged and empowered employees want to help. Let them! No nurse generally comes to work with adverse intention. Positive leader and employee relationships can be developed. Providing opportunities for employees to share feelings, thoughts, and ideas can be powerful. However, leaders must listen and be present for others to feel heard.

A colleague shared a successful idea that she deployed in her work environment when employees presented an issue. The white board in her office says the following:

- A "free &*$!@" in which employees are allowed to come in and complain about something. With this option, they get what is bothering them off their chests and nothing more is said.

- The second option is to bring a problem forward for discussion along with possible solutions. The leader and employee work together to come up with a viable solution(s) to the problem.

- The final option is the employee brings the problem to the leader, has no solution(s), and the leader takes over the problem. In this option, the employee supports the leader's decision for solution, regardless of whether the employee agrees it was the right approach.

This problem-solving process has worked well and provides a sense of empowerment to employees because they know they have options and full leadership support.

PRACTICE PEARLS

- Follow your instincts and trust yourself.
- Take the time to decrease stress and harness energy for positive outcomes.
- Empower others to assist in getting things done.
- Value yourself and those around you.

One of the most important tools that you can utilize to mitigate stress is communication. Leaders must communicate often and effectively. Some types of communication, such as delivering bad news, can be difficult but are essential for leadership success. Other communiqués, such as providing information via a short email or posting a notice, are simple. More complex communication may entail holding frequent staff meetings; this might be repetitive at different times and on different days, but the strategy is meant to ensure important messages are getting to each employee and being heard firsthand. Regardless of the type of communication, it is all essential. The well-informed and involved employee will be less stressed and develop trusting relationships with others and most importantly, with the leader. Trust what you believe in as a leader. Value those around you to shape that vision.

PRACTICE PEARLS

- Communication is key.
- Communicate often and in different formats.
- Communication needs to include everyone.

CONCLUSION

Being a leader takes courage. Learning about applying leadership in any nursing role is essential and it is interesting. As described, there is no single definition of leadership but a collection of characteristics identifying excellence in leadership practice. All nurses should be viewed as having the opportunity to be leaders: in their specialty, with their peers, in their work unit, among their assigned patient group, and with friends and family. Taking ownership and feeling a sense of responsibility or control minimizes stress, subsequent fatigue, and the potential for burnout. The next chapter discusses professional integrity, associated dilemmas, and the nuances that facilitate connections among stress, fatigue, and burnout.

REFERENCES

Carlson, J. (2009). A retiring bunch. *Modern Healthcare, 39*(26), 6.

Cox, D. (2002). *Leadership when the heat is on.* Chicago, IL: McGraw-Hill.

Donabedian, A. (1980). *Explorations in quality assessment and monitoring: The definition of quality and approaches to assessment.* Ann Arbor, MI: Health Administration Press.

Dudiy, S. (2005). *Top nine tips for better teamwork and team building.* Retrieved from http://www.time-management-guide.com/teamwork-tips.html

Glaser, J., & Hess, R. (2011). Leveraging health care IT to improve operational performance. *Healthcare Financial Management, 65*(2), 82–85.

Greenleaf Center for Servant Leadership. (n.d.). *What is servant leadership?* Retrieved from https://greenleaf.org/what-is-servant-leadership

Grossman, S. C., & Valiga, T. M. (2009). *The new leadership challenge: Creating a future for nursing.* Philadelphia, PA: F. A. Davis.

Guyton, N. (2012). Nine principles of successful nursing leadership. *American Nurse Today, 7*(8). Retrieved from http://www.americannursetoday.com/nine-principles-of-successful-nursing-leadership

Lieberson, S., & O'Connor, J. F. (1972). Leadership and organizational performance: A study of large corporations. *American Sociological Review, 37*(2), 117–130.

Marion, R., & Uhl-Bien, M. (2001). *Leadership in complex organizations.* (Report 11). Retrieved from http://digitalcommons.unl.edu/cgi/viewcontent.cgi?article=1012&context=managementfacpub

Mills, D. Q. (2005). The importance of leadership. In *Leadership: How to lead, how to live* (Chapter 1). Waltham, MA: MindEdge Press.

Nauert, R. (n.d.). Employee satisfaction key for customer satisfaction. *PsychCentral.* Retrieved from http://psychcentral.com/news/2011/06/02/employee-satisfaction-key-for-customer-satisfaction/26623.html

Nikravan, L. (2012). Why creativity is the most important leadership quality. *Chief Learning Officer.* Retrieved from http://www.clomedia.com/articles/why-creativity-is-the-most-important-leadership-quality

Noudelman, A. (2015). 7 signs of weak leadership. *LinkedIn Pulse.* Retrieved from https://www.linkedin.com/pulse/7-signs-weak-leadership-aleksandr-noudelman

Online BSN. (2009, September 14). 25 most famous nurses in history. *Nurseblogger.* Retrieved from http://onlinebsn.org/2009/25-most-famous-nurses-in-history/

Shirey, M. R. (2006). Stress and coping in nurse managers: Two decades of research. *Nursing Economics, 24*(4), 193. Retrieved from http://www.medscape.com/viewarticle/543837

Waddill-Goad, S. (2013). *The development of a Leadership Fatigue questionnaire* (doctoral dissertation). American Sentinel University, Aurora, Colorado.

5

PROFESSIONAL INTEGRITY

Suzanne Waddill-Goad, DNP, MBA, RN, CEN
Rita Haxton, DNP, RN, NEA-BC

OBJECTIVES

- Consider how nursing is changing and how that affects the stress levels of nurses.

- Consider how diversity (ethnic culture, tenure, age, and so on) in nursing is positive for the profession.

- Consider what it means to be a "professional" nurse.

- Explore how different nursing roles lead to different burnout rates.

- Explore how to avoid boundary crossings.

- Consider how to manage stress while on the job.

Nursing is the nation's largest healthcare profession (Health Resources and Services Administration [HRSA], 2010). According to a report from HRSA, 2.6 million of all registered nurses, or 84.8%, are actively employed in nursing. The majority of nurses, 62.2%, work in a hospital setting, according to the 2010 Institute of Medicine (IOM) report on the future of nursing.

THE FUTURE OF NURSING

Nursing care is the core business in hospitals because people seldom are hospitalized unless they need nursing care and observation. If healthcare continues to change as is being predicted, the percentage of nurses working in the inpatient hospital setting will decline as the nation begins to shift from an acute-care focus to prevention and better chronic-disease management. The only patients who will remain in the hospital will be complex patients and those patients who are no longer acute but do not have a safe place for transfer.

Nurses will continue to be needed for those patients whose complex medical needs require hospitalization. The overall need for nurses is not expected to decline due to a "graying of the population" and the increase of patients with chronic disease. The focus on population health will expand the use of nurses in the outpatient, transitional, and home settings. Many of the changes to come are unknown and may produce anxiety and an underlying stress for nurses.

The Institute of Medicine (IOM) report on the future of nursing describes the major roles and responsibilities of nurses in the following major areas: direct patient care to teach and counsel patients; coordinate care and advocate for patients; and research and evaluate more effective ways of caring for patients (IOM, 2010). Even though one of the major responsibilities of nursing is direct patient care, nurses spend 80%

of their time on documentation, medication administration, and communication with other providers. This leaves less than 20% of their time specifically for providing other types of direct care (IOM, 2010).

The IOM report can be found at http://iom.nationalacademies.org/ Reports/2010/The-Future-of-Nursing-Leading-Change-Advancing-Health.aspx.

With implementation of the Affordable Care Act (ACA) in 2010, the United States has an opportunity to move to a higher-quality, safer, more affordable healthcare system by transforming the way healthcare is currently provided. The ACA is the biggest change in healthcare since the creation of Medicare and Medicaid in 1965. The nursing profession has the potential to play a major role in changes by virtue of the number of nurses, their adaptive capacity, and the versatility of nursing.

PRACTICE PEARL

"Now is a critical time for nursing to step forward to bridge the gap between coverage and access; to coordinate the complex care of patients with chronic illnesses; for advanced practice nurses to work to the full capability of their license potential as primary care providers; and finally to see the value of nurses and enable their contribution across all practice settings and the healthcare continuum." (IOM, 2010)

Due to the close relationship of nurses with patients and their scientific knowledge of care processes across the continuum, nurses have an opportunity and ability to act as partners with all healthcare professionals and to lead the redesign of the healthcare environment (IOM, 2010). The challenge for nurses will be to learn how best to balance the needs of patients without increasing their own stress and fatigue. Stress in nursing has been discussed since the 1950s; four main sources of anxiety remain among nurses: patient care, decision-making, taking responsibility, and change (Jennings, 2008).

Inherent stress in the role of a nurse is related to the physical labor of nursing, working long hours (as well as rotating shifts), constantly dealing with human suffering, and complex interpersonal relationships with patients, families, and fellow healthcare staff (Jennings, 2008). With increasing pressure to focus on cost efficiencies, improved quality of care, increasing the use of technology, and increasing expectations by patients and families, nurses will continue to feel the pressure to change the way they practice. Undoubtedly, this pressure will result in feelings of anxiety, stress, fatigue, and burnout for some nurses.

PRACTICE PEARLS

- Be willing to ask for help.
- Develop supportive relationships with nursing peers, leaders, and other co-workers to reduce stress in your work environment.
- Help to develop a supportive team environment with other clinical colleagues.

DIVERSITY IN NURSING

The U.S. Department of Health and Human Services, Health Resources and Services Administration (HRSA) is the department of the government whose primary mission is to help ensure access to care for all Americans. One of its roles is to evaluate the adequacy of the number of healthcare providers by category and the distribution across the nation to meet the demand for access to care (HRSA, 2015). Diversity in nursing is an important goal; the nursing education community is working to ensure the nursing profession demographics match the needs of the population for accessible, affordable, and quality healthcare.

A report published by HRSA compared diversity in healthcare occupations (within the health workforce) to the diversity of the current U.S. working-age population (16 years of age or older who are currently employed or seeking employment). With the exception of nursing being a predominantly female profession, the ethnic distribution was very similar to the current working population of the United States. This report shows progress by universities in their work to improve diversity in nursing.

Table 5.1 shows a summarized table of percentages from the report, which highlights the diversity by sex and race of registered nurses in comparison to the U.S. working-age population (HRSA, 2015).

TABLE 5.1 DIVERSITY: AN HRSA-BASED COMPARISON BETWEEN NURSING AND THE U.S. WORKING POPULATION

	Male	Female	White	Black	Asian	American Indian	Pacific Islander	Multiple/Other Race Affiliation
U.S. Working-Age Population (%)	52.8	47.2	77.6	13.6	6.0	0.7	0.2	2.0
Registered Nurses (%)	9.2	90.8	78.6	10.7	8.8	0.4	0.1	1.4

The increase in diversity and a greater willingness to practice in underserved areas have resulted in improved access to care by healthcare providers who are culturally and linguistically skilled to provide appropriate services (National Advisory Council on Nurse Education and Practice [NACNEP], 2013). Most of the research on improving patient outcomes for minority populations has been done with independent providers. The role of nursing is important in diversity because of the personal relationship that occurs between a nurse and a patient. Properly matching patient and care providers relative to race and language creates what is referred to as *concordance*. By having race and language concordance, communication between the patient and care provider improves, resulting in better patient satisfaction and outcomes of care (National Research Council [NRC], 2004).

DEFINITION OF PROFESSIONAL NURSING

Healthcare used to be defined by the care provided by physicians when they diagnosed and treated a disease. This perspective caused confusion for nurses and other clinical professions who struggled to define their professional role. Nurses have since demonstrated their differentiated skills and specialized knowledge, thus distancing their professional role from physicians and other clinical professions.

In the early development of an understanding or definition of nursing, the discussion must begin with Florence Nightingale, whose writings began in 1860. She described nursing's activities as something that put patients in the best condition possible for nature to take its course (Nightingale, 1860). Over 100 years later, the landmark definition of nursing was contained in the statute of the New York State Practice Act of 1972, which has served as legal support for nurses' independent practice and become a model for other states to use in their nurse practice acts. The definition enables nurses to claim a body of knowledge apart from medicine and to have authority over their own practice.

Here is the definition of registered nursing from the New York State Education Department, Office of Health Professions:

> "The practice of the profession of nursing, as a registered professional nurse, is defined as diagnosing and treating human responses to actual or potential health problems through such services as case finding, health teaching, health counseling, and provision of supportive care to or restorative of life and well-being, and executing medical regimens prescribed by a licensed physician, dentist, or other licensed healthcare provider legally authorized under this title and in accordance with the commissioner's regulations. A nursing regimen shall be consistent with and shall not vary any existing medical regimen." New York State Education Department (NYSED), Article 139 Nursing, definition of the practice of nursing (2015)

The New York State law began the movement in nursing to develop nursing diagnoses that describe a patient's response to health problems. In follow-up to this movement, the American Nurses Association (ANA) developed and published "Nursing: A Social Policy Statement," which describes nurses' responsibilities to patients and society; this further validates the advocacy role of nurses (ANA, 2010).

Here is the ANA's depiction of what *nursing* is: Nursing's Social Policy Statement, Role of the Nursing Profession, is as follows:

> "The protection, promotion, and optimization of health and abilities, prevention of illness and injury, alleviation of suffering through the diagnosis and treatment of human response, and advocacy in the care of individuals, families, communities, and populations." ANA, (2015)

Mason (2011), in her discussion of the definition of nursing, gives a summary of Patricia Benner's position relative to caring in nursing. Nurses must:

- Continue to have a demand for an expert knowledge level
- Possess the ability to integrate physical, psychological, emotional, and social dimensions of health
- Demonstrate skill in administering supportive care
- Exude superb critical thinking and clinical judgment
- Hone their assessment skills
- Be proficient in coordinating care and advocacy

Incidentally, Benner has continued to study nursing practice over the last 25 years since her landmark study was published in 1984, where nursing practice has changed dramatically during this time.

Currently, great challenges exist within nursing practice to appropriately delegate care to unlicensed personnel and deliver care in challenging environments to far more complex patients. This can also be a source of stress, especially for nurses who want to "do it all". However, for the most cost-effective care and efficiency of care provision, care should be assigned based on education, skill, and licensure. And of course, there are some provisions that only a licensed registered nurse can perform. A joint statement on delegation (in a white paper) from the American Nurses Association (ANA) and the National Council of State Boards of Nursing (NCSBN) can be found at https://www.ncsbn.org/ Delegation_joint_statement_NCSBN-ANA.pdf.

In the nursing profession, challenges occur not only with transition of novice nurses to competent practice but with the transition from competent to expert levels of practice. In addition, frequent job changes may also prevent nurses from reaching the expert level of practice in their specialty (Benner, Tanner, & Chesla, 2009). Stress also increases for experienced nurses when there are few competent peers to serve as mentors or coaches for less experienced nurses.

Over the past hundred years, the definition of nursing has been refined to reflect the development of a body of knowledge specific to nursing. Nursing has had a long and important legacy in healthcare. One of the most important roles is as an advocate for a better, safer, more humanistic healthcare system. It is important that nursing continue this legacy into the future with the highest standards of professional integrity and a focus of providing patient-centered healthcare.

VARIOUS ROLES IN NURSING

With the aging of society and the increase in chronic health conditions in the population, healthcare systems are dealing with an increasing number of medically complex patients. Nursing is one of the major professions stepping forward to take on additional responsibilities. In the rapidly changing healthcare environment, nursing will continue to evolve as a profession with new and stimulating opportunities. Caring for higher acuity patients will be more challenging for hospitals while organizations continue to receive smaller reimbursement. Nurses may be able to take on more responsibilities in hospitals, clinics, and care centers to help meet these new challenges.

One of the strengths of the nursing profession is the ability of nurses to work in multiple and different roles in healthcare. Feeling stressed in one area? Make a move to another area! Although over 60% of nurses work in a hospital setting, many nurses have moved beyond the hospital to private practice, home health, hospice, long-term care, outpatient surgical centers, insurance companies, managed care companies, industry, nursing education, and more (HRSA, 2010). In the hospital setting, there are also many direct and indirect nursing roles such as critical care, emergency, surgical services (same day, sterile processing, operating room, post-anesthesia recovery, etc.), medical, pediatrics, mother and baby units, labor and delivery, care management, utilization review, leadership, and education specialists. On occasions, jobs are even created by nurses who discover a problem and develop a solution that improves the delivery of care for patients.

When a nurse decides to pursue advanced nursing or non-nursing education and/or become certified in a specialty, she or he has the opportunity to become a leader in healthcare. The advanced practice nurse has an expanded scope of practice, which helps to fill a void relative to access and care for patients. The increased number of advanced practice nurses has opened another world for nursing to provide primary and preventive care. In many states, an advanced practice nurse's scope is expanded to the specialties of certified midwives, nurse anesthetists, and family nurse practitioners, as well as nurse practitioners in cardiology, oncology, neonatal, and many other advanced clinical specialties. Professional nursing organizations have taken an active role state by state to increase the independence of the advanced practice role. In some states, nurses are allowed to practice independently, but in other states they must have a collaborative relationship with a sponsoring physician. In addition to advanced practice specialties in clinical areas, there are also opportunities in leadership and education.

Registered nurses work collaboratively with all other healthcare professionals. Nursing has practice restrictions according to the scope of practice defined by each state's board of nursing. The practice rules are usually established by the state legislature delegating oversight by the state board of nursing. Nursing is generally not allowed to operate or practice independently. Nurses implement medical provider and other clinicians (licensed independent practitioners) orders so many times, people believe that nurses always operate under another provider's license. Each nurse is responsible for providing care under his or her own license. With more than four times as many nurses as physicians in the United States, nursing provides direct patient care ordered by providers, such as medication administration, dressing changes, dialysis treatments, and so on (American Association of Colleges of Nursing [AACN], 2011). There is opportunity for the nurse to master complex, multifaceted issues that affect our healthcare systems and the health problems in the population at large. The nursing role has expanded beyond the performance of tasks and procedures—nurses are effective collaborators in a multidisciplinary health team who help patients to navigate the complex health environment (Tiffon, 2013).

DEFINING BOUNDARIES

Since 1999, when Gallup first included nurses in the survey for ethics and honesty, nurses have ranked the highest with over 80% of survey participants; they have been ranked first every year with the exception of 2001, when firefighters were on top after the horrific terrorist attack on 9/11 (Riffkin, 2014). The results of the survey reflect a special relationship or bond that is built between nurses and patients. Patients expect that a nurse will act in their best interest and will respect their dignity. Nurses have the privilege to care for patients when they are not at their best and often are the most vulnerable. Nurses' integrity and ethics must always stay at the highest level.

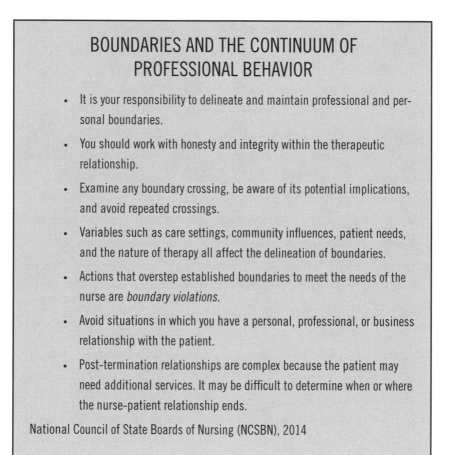

BOUNDARIES AND THE CONTINUUM OF PROFESSIONAL BEHAVIOR

- It is your responsibility to delineate and maintain professional and personal boundaries.
- You should work with honesty and integrity within the therapeutic relationship.
- Examine any boundary crossing, be aware of its potential implications, and avoid repeated crossings.
- Variables such as care settings, community influences, patient needs, and the nature of therapy all affect the delineation of boundaries.
- Actions that overstep established boundaries to meet the needs of the nurse are *boundary violations.*
- Avoid situations in which you have a personal, professional, or business relationship with the patient.
- Post-termination relationships are complex because the patient may need additional services. It may be difficult to determine when or where the nurse-patient relationship ends.

National Council of State Boards of Nursing (NCSBN), 2014

According to the NCSBN, nursing is defined via professional boundaries whose scope includes "the spaces between the nurse's power and the client's vulnerability. The power of the nurse comes from the nurse's professional position and access to sensitive personal information. The difference in personal information the nurse knows about the patient versus personal information the patient knows about the nurse creates an imbalance in the nurse-patient relationship" (NCSBN, 2014, p. 4). The NCSBN has published a pamphlet identifying professional standards to help nurses understand professional boundaries and work to establish and maintain those boundaries (NCSBN, 2014).

When a successful relationship develops between a nurse and patient, it is based on trust, compassion, and mutual respect. Such a positive relationship between a patient and nurse has been shown to improve patient outcomes (Duffy & Brewer, 2011). The goal is to develop a therapeutic relationship that "allows nurses to apply their professional knowledge, skills, abilities and experiences toward meeting the health needs of the patient" (NCSBN, 2014, p. 4). When this type of relationship occurs, the patient's dignity is protected, and it allows for the development of trust and respect between the nurse and the patient.

PRACTICE PEARLS

- Think about what you need to do your *best* work and be willing to ask for it.
- Be trustworthy.
- Learn about professional boundaries and the consequences of violations.
- Be on the safe side and never post work-related information on social media.

Environmental chaos, potentiated by a suboptimal work culture, can cause undue stress for nurses. Healthy work cultures may produce results that are just the opposite. The negative results of an unhealthy work culture may inhibit a nurse's ability to focus on the very reasons he or she chose to be a nurse: to create an effective nurse-patient relationship and to feel as if his or her time is making a difference. Nurses must learn to prioritize and remain objective and organized in their approach to care provision, leadership, or education to prevent undue stress, resulting fatigue, and the potential progression for burnout.

Behaviors considered inappropriate can be separated into three categories: boundary crossings, boundary violations, and sexual misconduct.

BOUNDARY CROSSING

The NCSBN defines a *boundary crossing* as a decision to deviate from an established boundary for a therapeutic purpose (NCSBN, 2014). Boundary crossing occurs when a nurse goes beyond a therapeutic relationship. A boundary crossing is usually a brief excursion across a professional boundary that may be inadvertent, thoughtless, or even purposeful. It is usually justified by the nurse as meeting a therapeutic care need.

For example, a nurse could disclose personal information to reassure a patient. When this occurs, the nurse should consider this a cautionary flag and should closely consider whether this was the right thing to do. The following two cases describe situations where boundaries were crossed.

Case 1: A neonatal intensive care unit (NICU) nurse became especially attached to a premature infant. The family was from out of town. The parents had several other children so they were not able to come into town to see the infant very often. The nurse felt that she knew what the baby needed more than the parents since she was frequently at the hospital. When the baby was getting close to being discharged, the parents came to the hospital and stayed for a couple of days to learn the baby's post-discharge care needs. However, the nurse did not believe the parents were ready for the baby to be discharged, so she asked the physician to delay it for several days. She also got into an argument with one of the other nurses in the NICU because the other nurse believed the parents' knowledge was adequate for discharge. In this example, the nurse became too involved with the baby and should not have requested a delayed (and potentially much more costly) hospital stay due to her feelings about the parents' ability to care for their child.

Case 2: A young adult male patient was admitted to a surgical floor after a somewhat complicated appendectomy. The nurse caring for the patient was very compassionate and provided good care. However, she spent more time with this patient than her others—he was a young, good-looking college student. The nurse was just slightly older than the student and she knew he was from another state and had no family in the area. She overstepped her boundaries in wanting to help him when she gave him her personal cell phone number and offered to give him a ride home when he was discharged. In addition, they began a texting relationship while he was still a patient in the hospital. The nurse should not have divulged her personal contact information or developed a texting relationship while the patient was still under hospital care.

BOUNDARY VIOLATIONS

A *boundary violation* should be considered a danger flag. For example, if a nurse believes a pediatric patient's parents are not ready to safely care for the patient, the nurse must be sure objectivity reigns—if the nurse's relationship with the patient is "too close," his or her judgment may be clouded. The following case describes a situation where a nurse crossed a professional boundary.

Case 3: A pediatric patient was admitted for a serious respiratory illness. The parents of the patient were young, and this was their first child. The nurse caring for the child had a number of years of experience as a nurse and three children of her own. During the course of the child's illness, the nurse witnessed a number of instances when she felt the parents were not attending to the child's needs (showing up late for meetings with the doctor, not responding appropriately when the child needed comforting, and so on). She wondered what would happen to the child when he was discharged from the hospital. Could or would the parents properly care for the sick child? In her haste to do "something" to remedy the situation, she called the State Child Protective Services Agency on one of her days off from home to report the situation. Unfortunately, it did not meet the outlined criteria for reporting. However, the agency was obligated to investigate. Once the hospital was advised of the report (during the investigation), hospital leaders felt that education was necessary for staff. An educational program was provided for all staff to differentiate the licensing duty to report and the differences between the obligation and an emotional reaction to observations of parent-child interactions. In this case, the nurse overstepped her boundaries by not knowing the difference between what she was obligated to report and how she felt about the child's parents and their parenting skills. The nurse did not get into any trouble per se, but it did raise questions about her professional competency.

SEXUAL MISCONDUCT

The last category, *sexual misconduct*, is the most serious violation. A nurse has the responsibility and duty to make sure this line is never crossed until the nurse-patient relationship has ended (Hanna & Suplee, 2012). It is the nurse's responsibility to understand the laws and practice regulations that apply to boundary violations in his or her state of practice. The following case outlines an example of sexual misconduct.

Case 4: An adult male patient was admitted for a major surgical procedure. While he was hospitalized, he was very overt about flirting with all of the nurses that he encountered. For some nurses, it made them so uncomfortable they requested not to be assigned to his case. For others, they enjoyed the attention and flirted right back with the patient. However, one nurse took the flirting too far. When propositioned by the patient for sexual favors, she obliged. She thought she was doing nothing wrong and truly intended to help the patient in his recovery. Seemingly, she was unaware of her professional responsibilities and the boundaries outlined by law relative to the practice of nursing. The nurse should not have engaged in any sexual banter or contact with this patient. The hospital felt it was obligated to report the incident to its legal counsel and the Board of Nursing (BON). After investigation and a comprehensive review, her employment was terminated. The BON performed its own investigation and levied the appropriate consequences.

Clear sexual boundaries are crucial for patient safety (NCSBN, 2009). Violations of this type can leave lasting repercussions for the nurse, the facility, and the patient. A comprehensive guide was published to assist BONs in their education and case review by the NCSBN in 2009 and can be found at https://www.ncsbn.org/Sexual_Misconduct_Book_web.pdf. In addition, the following information has been excerpted from the report:

> In the National Council of State Boards of Nursing's analysis of 10 years of Nursys® data (NCSBN, 2009), 53,361 nurses were disciplined; of those, 636, or 0.57%, were included in the following categories: sexual misconduct, sex with client, sexual abuse, sexual language or sexual boundaries. Therefore, sexual misconduct is not a common complaint to a Board of Nursing (BON). The actual prevalence, however, is not known. Indeed, 38 to 52% of health care professionals report knowing of colleagues who have been sexually involved with patients (Halter et al., 2007; NCSBN, 2009).

MANAGING STRESS AND PERSONAL BEHAVIOR

Nurses learn about nursing boundaries when, as students, they recite the "Nightingale Pledge" used in pinning ceremonies throughout the country. Some passages from the "Nightingale Pledge" that specifically address professional boundaries are "I will abstain from whatever is deleterious and mischievous…maintain and elevate the standard of my profession…will hold confidence matters committed to my keeping… in the practice of my calling…and devote myself to the welfare of those committed to my care" (Gretter, 1893).

These are important descriptions of the boundaries relating to the responsibilities of a nurse. The pledge was created by Gretter and a committee for the Farrand Training School as a modified Hippocratic Oath for nurses (as a token of esteem for the founder of modern nursing) (Gretter, 1893). It is amazing to realize the intelligence and forethought, see the current relevance to today's practice, and note that the highest ethical standards have not changed in 150 years.

Due to the personal and intimate nature of caring in a nurse's professional role, nurses may be conflicted and may make moral judgments about a particular course of treatment for a patient (Cavaliere, Daly, Dowling, & Montgomery, 2010). This might cause the nurse to drift into inappropriate boundary decisions. It is not unusual for nurses to experience moral distress from situations surrounding end-of-life care decisions, institutional policy constraints, and situations that the nurse may believe affect his/her ability to provide quality care to patients (Roberts, Grubb, & Grosch, 2012). The situation that caused the moral distress (and the moral distress itself) may result in increased stress. This way adds to already existing fatigue and leads to symptoms of burnout.

Stress often leads to unintended consequences, including inappropriate behavior. Although nurses learn about healthy behavior and ways to cope with stress in their formal academic programs, the realities of practice may be challenging. The use of prescription drugs in the U.S. population is a grave public health concern and is reported in some fashion nearly every day by a variety of media sources. Unfortunately, healthcare providers are not immune; estimates of diversion and use among healthcare workers is suspected to be on the rise, but reliable statistics about prevalence are shrouded in clandestine secrecy (New, 2015).

Prescription drug abuse is on the rise among nurses (Brosher, 2014). Jason (2015) posited in her series of articles to better acquaint licensees with the Oregon Board of Nursing's requirements that there was a dearth of knowledge regarding impairment in the nursing population at large. Based on her research of the available data (including sources at the ANA), estimates may be upward of 10% of nurses using alcohol or drugs to an extent sufficient to impair performance; they could also pose a risk to the public. This number does not include nurses who might be impaired due to mental issues. Most healthcare organizations are aware of the potential for diversion of controlled substances and other pharmacologics; however, the degree to which they actively monitor healthcare workers varies. To learn more about diversion and its consequences, this link provides a presentation from Kimberly New, a nationally known speaker and consultant: https://www.ncsbn.org/0613_DISC_Kim_New.pdf.

The ANA also has a resource center for impaired nurses that can be found on its web page: http://www.nursingworld.org/MainMenu Categories/WorkplaceSafety/Healthy-Work-Environment/ Work-Environment/ImpairedNurse.

The greatest risk of nursing drug diversion is public safety: community and/or patient harm (Jason, 2015). Diversion in a healthcare setting is a criminal activity (New, 2015); institutions have a duty to provide a safe care environment. A nurse on his or her very best day can make a mistake. Impairment exponentially raises the likelihood of an error. Due to the seriousness of the nature of diversion, some state agencies are considering formal programs requiring standardized organizational surveillance. In addition, regulatory agencies have taken note. Not only is there organizational regulatory liability and penalty potential, but the licensee faces a host of costly adverse consequences that could include civil penalties and negative publicity (New, 2015). Additionally, the professional healthcare worker may lose his or her license to practice.

One way to avoid crossing professional boundary lines is by increasing education of nurses regarding violations. It is important for nurses to know how to identify early warning signs of professional boundary crossing and the resulting potential or real harm that may occur to patients, as well as the impact on other nursing staff (Holder & Schenthal, 2007). Nurses have professional responsibility to themselves, their peers, and their patients. Nurse practice acts in all states require nurses to mandatorily report unprofessional, illegal, and unsafe practices.

Many consider professional boundary crossing an occupational hazard in nursing. Human interactions put nurses at risk if they don't have a clear understanding of their role and responsibility. Nurses are encouraged to develop caring relationships with patients, and patient satisfaction is often a direct measure of factors based on the relationship. Nurses and other medical professionals need to spend time to learn about professional boundary risks in formalized educational settings and in the work environment.

Incidents that come under public scrutiny in the media are generally stories of victim abuse or malpractice. These examples often result in mistrust and wariness between patients and nurses, negatively affecting the nurse-patient relationship. When an allegation surfaces or an actual violation occurs, the issues are generally referred to the state board of nursing for investigation. The state boards of nursing are the regulatory agencies responsible for protecting the public. The protection is established by a set of statutes, rules, and regulations that make up each individual state's Nurse Practice Act. The Nurse Practice Act is the basis to determine appropriateness of a nurse's actions (Holder & Schenthal, 2007).

A significant problem with alleged or actual boundary transgressions is they are often committed by well-educated professionals during a stressful situation. These transgressions are rarely deliberate exploitation, but a consequence of well-intentioned actions where a nurse rationalizes crossing professional boundaries for the benefit of the patient. Proactive consideration must be given to preventing boundary violations. Frequently, they begin with innocent boundary drift such as thoughts about what could be done to help a patient in a difficult situation. Boundary drift may progress to boundary crossing and even slip into a violation. Ideally, education to prevent boundary violation needs to occur before boundaries start to drift.

Managing appropriate professional boundaries is each healthcare professional's responsibility. The best prevention is the development of a strong awareness and education plan. This education must include definitions of professional boundaries, differentiation of boundary crossings, and examples of violations. Each professional has a "violation potential." Understanding how to assess and address your own and others' violation potential can help to prevent boundary crossings.

Violation potential is dynamic and can change over time in response to life events and personal vulnerabilities. Nurses must be aware of the risk. Risk factors are adversely affected by unresolved trauma from childhood, experiencing family or close friends who have died, a critical illness, and stress in general. Environmental elements include work setting, patient type, and a nurse's experience. A person's violation potential can be increased by an unexpected stress catalyst such as a divorce, death, or career change. This may cause a well-intentioned nurse to cross the line that separates ethical from unethical behavior (Holder & Schenthal, 2007).

Support from nursing leaders, colleagues, and peers for strategies to address the inherent environmental chaos, stressful events, and subsequent feelings of stress must be a priority in the healthcare environment. Employee assistance programs (EAP) and human resource (HR) personnel can be excellent resources for those struggling with personal or professional stress.

PRACTICE PEARLS

- Pay attention to the consequences of stress in the work environment.
- Use available organizational resources when necessary to assist with stress management (EAP or HR).
- Be supportive to others who are stressed.

CONCLUSION

The nursing profession has become increasingly diverse in the following areas: age, years of professional experience, gender, and ethnicity. This diversity should be viewed as positive for the profession. Diversity brings a wide variety of experiences, styles of thinking, and frames of reference. We know change is afoot and new thinking is required to thrive in the healthcare systems of the future. Being a stellar professional in practice, educational preparation, and behavior is necessary for today's nurse. Nurses must become tolerant of the chaos in healthcare; a heightened awareness of environmental stressors leading to feelings of stress, the propensity for fatigue, and the potential for burnout must be paramount. The following chapter will explore the implications of silos in healthcare.

REFERENCES

American Association of Colleges of Nursing (AACN). (2011, April 12). *Nursing fact sheet.* Retrieved from http://www.aacn.nche.edu/media-relations/fact-sheets/nursing-fact-sheet

American Nurses Association (ANA). (2010). *Nursing: A social policy statement.* Silver Spring, MD: Author.

American Nurses Association (ANA). (2015). *What is nursing?* Retrieved from http://nursingworld.org/EspeciallyForYou/What-is-Nursing.

Benner, P. (1984). *From novice to expert: Excellence in clinical nursing practice.* Upper Saddle River, NJ: Prentice Hall Health.

Benner, P., Tanner, C., & Chesla, C. (2009). *Expertise in nursing practice* (2nd ed.). New York, NY: Springer Publishing Company.

Brosher, B. (2014, August). Prescription drug abuse among nurses a growing problem. Indiana public media news. Retrieved from http://indianapublicmedia.org/news/prescription-drug-abuse-nurses-growing-problem-71203/.

Cavaliere, T., Daly, B., Dowling, D., & Montgomery, K. (2010). Moral distress in neonatal intensive care units RNs. *Advanced Neonatal Care, 10*(3), 145–156. doi: 10.1097/ANC.0b013e3181dd6c48

Duffy, J., & Brewer, B. (2011). Feasibility of a multi-institutional collaborative to improve patient-nurse relationship quality. *Journal of Nursing Administration, 41*(2), 78–83.

Gretter, L. (1893). *The Florence Nightingale Pledge.* Retrieved from http://nursing-world.org/HIstory/FlorenceNightingalePledge

Hanna, A., & Suplee, P. (2012, September). Don't cross the line: Respecting professional boundaries. *Nursing 2012, 42*(9), 40–47.

Health Resources and Services Administration (HRSA). (2010, September). *The registered nurse population: Findings from the 2008 national sample survey of registered nurses.* Washington, DC: U.S. Department of Health and Human Services.

Health Resources and Services Administration (HRSA). (2015, January). *Sex, race and ethnic diversity of U.S. healthcare occupations (2010–2012).* Retrieved from http://bhpr.hrsa.gov/healthworkforce/supplydemand/usworkforce/diversityushealthoccupations.pdf

Holder, K., & Schenthal, S. (2007). Watch your step: Nursing and professional boundaries. *Nursing Management, 38*(2), 24–29.

Institute of Medicine (IOM). (2010). *The future of nursing: Leading change advancing health.* Retrieved from http://www.nursingworld.org/MainMenuCategories/ThePracticeofProfessionalNursing/workforce/IOM-Future-of-Nursing-Report-1

Jason, R. R. (2015). Monitoring the impaired provider. *Oregon State Board of Nursing Sentinel, 34*(1), 6–10. Retrieved from http://epubs.democratprinting.com/article/Monitoring+The+Impaired+Provider/1963682/0/article.html

Jennings, B. (2008). Work stress and burnout among nurses: Role of the work environment and working conditions. In R. G. Hughes (Ed.), *Patient safety and quality: An evidence-based handbook for nurses* (pp. 133–158). Rockville, MD: Agency for Healthcare Research and Quality.

Mason, D. (2011). *The nursing profession: Development, challenges and opportunities.* San Francisco, CA: Jossey-Bass.

National Advisory Council on Nurse Education and Practice (NACNEP). (2013). *Achieving health equity through nursing workforce diversity.* Retrieved from http://www.hrsa.gov/advisorycommittees/bhwadvisory/nacnep/reports/eleventhreport.pdf

National Council of State Boards of Nursing (NCSBN). (2014). *A nurse's guide to professional boundaries.* Chicago, IL: Author.

National Council of State Boards of Nursing (NCSBN). (2009). *Practical guidelines for boards of nursing on sexual misconduct cases.* Retrieved from https://www.ncsbn.org/Sexual_Misconduct_Book_web.pdf

National Research Council (NRC). (2004). *In the nation's compelling interest: Ensuring diversity in the health professionals.* Washington, DC: National Academies Press.

New, K. (2015). Preventing, detecting, and investigating drug diversion in health care facilities. *Missouri State Board of Nursing Newsletter, 16*(4), 11–14.

Nightingale, F. (1860). *Notes on nursing: What it is and what it is not.* London, UK: D. Appleton and Company, reprinted by Dover Publications, New York, NY, 1969.

New York State Education Department (NYSED. (2015). *NYSOPnursing: Laws, rules &regulations: Article 139, section 6902.* New York State Office of Health Professions. Retrieved from http://www.op.nysed.gov/prof/nurse/article139.htm

Riffkin, R. (2014, December 18). *Americans rate nurses highest on honesty, ethical standards.* Retrieved from http://www.gallup.com/poll/180260/americans-rate-nurses-highest-honesty-ethical-standards.aspx

Roberts, R., Grubb, P., & Grosch, J. (2012, June 25). Alleviating job stress in nurses. *MedScape.* Retrieved from http://www.medscape.com/viewarticle/765974

Tiffon, C. (2013, March 1). Beyond the bedside: The changing role of today's nurse. *Huffington Post.* Retrieved from http://www.huffingtonpost.ccom/charles-tiffon-phd/nursing=school_b_1384285.html

6

THE INTERNAL STRAIN OF SILOS

Suzanne Waddill-Goad, DNP, MBA, RN, CEN
Holly Jo Langster, DNP, FNP-C, HCA, CENP

OBJECTIVES

- Understand the benefits and challenges of working as a team.

- Explore why the healthcare environment has become a mass of silos.

- Consider why the "silo" phenomenon is stress-inducing.

- Explore the different types of silos and how to combat them.

- Consider why competition for limited resources and personnel shortages lead to conflict among healthcare workers.

There is an infamous story about four people named Everybody, Somebody, Anybody, and Nobody. Although there doesn't seem be to a record of where the story originated, it resurfaces in the actual lives of healthcare professionals each day. The story goes like this:

> There was an important job to be done and Everybody was asked to do it. Everybody was sure Somebody would do it. Anybody could have done it, but Nobody did it. Somebody got angry about that because it was Everybody's job. Everybody thought Anybody could do it, but Nobody realized that Everybody wouldn't do it. It ended up that Everybody blamed Somebody when actually Nobody asked Anybody.

THE CHALLENGES OF WORKING AS A TEAM

Nursing is a team sport, and teamwork is critical. In 1965, Tuckman's research revealed four stages of team behavior: forming, storming, norming, and performing. This process is commonly used when launching new team or improvement efforts:

- *Forming* begins with the team members getting to know one another.

- *Storming* occurs after team members become comfortable and begin to take risks by sharing contrarian views.

- *Norming* occurs when the team exhibits cohesion and is working toward a common goal.

- *Performing* is reserved for what Tuckman called "high-performing teams" who are able to function as a unified group and without conflict.

Later in 1977, Tuckman and Jensen added *adjourning* to the team process, whereby the team uncouples or dissolves the group dynamics in an attempt to move on. This step has also been called *deforming* and *mourning*, due to the feelings team members experience when this phase of their work comes to an end.

Strong consideration should be given to the addition of teaching ideal teamwork and team behavior in formal nursing programs. Taking care of patients requires a multidisciplinary approach with a team of skilled individuals, all with their own area of expertise. While "everyone" is responsible for his or her own specialty, "everyone" also has to know how his or her work fits into the work of other disciplines.

Traditional organizational structures, especially in hospitals, have isolated clinical disciplines into silos. Nursing has often been organized in its own service line. Only recently have reorganizations integrated various clinical disciplines into a more unified and inclusive reporting structure. This reorganization has allowed an opportunity for enhanced collaboration and improved teamwork among specialties.

Isn't it true we sometimes find ourselves floundering through the day, wondering how we will ever get all of our work completed? A good analogy for being a nurse in today's complex healthcare environment is like standing in the middle of a tornado—where do you begin or which task needs to be accomplished first? Most nurses are good at prioritizing and can usually find the time to help a colleague in need. They can assist in task completion, make telephone calls to other disciplines, and provide patient care; however, when there is a sick call or when the daily plan doesn't unfold as expected, it can be quite challenging for the entire team to keep up with the work.

In an acute care setting, it becomes a bit more difficult, because hospitalized patients can be quite ill. Bedside nurses can sometimes team up and help each other out, but what they cannot do is complete each other's documentation. So even when teamed up for patient care activities, only part of the work can be done with a partner. Nurses in other roles, such as education or administration, can ask for help if they have teammates, but often they are solo acts left to their own resourcefulness to get way too much work done in one day's time.

Learning to prioritize is a key strategy to achieve your goals and feel a sense of accomplishment. At the end of a nurse's day, there is often work left undone. Sometimes we are aware there is work left needing to be completed. Other times, we don't discover it until an audit is completed or a lawsuit is filed and there is nothing in the record to support the efforts of the nurse or the care that was provided.

THE HEALTHCARE SILO PHENOMENON

Webster's dictionary (n.d.) defines *silo* as "a tower or pit on a farm used to store grain." If you've ever visited a farm, you know that only one type of grain is stored in a silo at a time. If, for instance, a farm harvests both corn and beans, the corn is kept in one silo while the beans are kept in another. A second definition for silo is "an underground chamber in which a guided missile is kept ready for firing." In both instances, the purpose of the silo is to isolate the item for its protection. To be siloed is to be *isolated*. When silos occur in healthcare, roles become isolated, disciplines become isolated, departments become isolated, communication becomes isolated, and frustrations often arise. Being frustrated with the work environment, work processes, and work colleagues is the beginning stage of stress and fatigue and may lead eventually to burnout.

Figure 6.1 shows some common silos found in the healthcare industry.

Silos

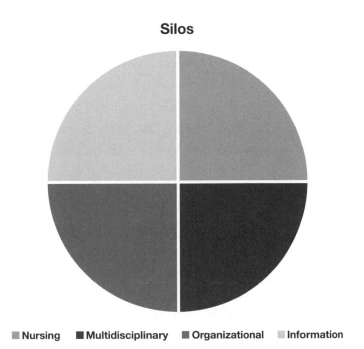

Nursing   Multidisciplinary   Organizational   Information

Figure 6.1   Healthcare silos are often a result of difficulties with communication and effective collaboration.

Healthcare has been known to have a number of inefficient work processes that have led to the creation of workarounds in the system. Workarounds are a prime offender for the establishment of silos. Silos result in difficulties with communication and effective collaboration. The person or persons who created the workaround are the only ones who know how it works. Communication, or the lack thereof, is a key contributing factor to errors in healthcare. Because healthcare is such a demanding field, nurses who learn workarounds are often praised as being resourceful and efficient. However, the new work process must be communicated so that others are aware and can comply.

One example of a workaround, likely to occur in a typical nurse's day, is related to securing enough intravenous medication pumps for post-operative patients. The post-operative unit might hoard and/or hide all the pumps they can find instead of following the hospital process of sending them back to the designated area for cleaning. This workaround is often a result of a day when the unit had a pump shortage. This approach might work for solving the unit's problem but can cause a real patient safety issue in other areas of the hospital. In addition, the pumps might not be cleaned as properly as they should (Tucker, 2009).

Silos occur in a multitude of ways. Much like the Everybody, Somebody, Anybody, and Nobody story, silos can lead to ineffective communication when a workaround might be put in place. A nurse might innocently create a workaround to accomplish his or her day's assigned work. This type of behavior makes it incredibly difficult to track workarounds that have been instituted, and they may inadvertently cause violations in standard practice and/or policy.

For instance, if nurses don't communicate with designated quality personnel, associated organizational metrics or quality indicators may never be achieved. Nurses in the acute care environment must be cognizant of compensable quality scoring. If there is improper, inaccurate, or missing documentation of the established quality indicators, inappropriate information may be publicly reported. Erroneous information may have a negative impact on financial reimbursement. This means money that's paid to hospitals through value-based purchasing plans might be less than expected, and the organization's reputation might negatively suffer in public reporting systems. System, people, and process communication are all *vital* to prevent silos from unintentionally damaging organizations. Today, informational knowledge is power, and communication is the way to unleash it.

PRACTICE PEARLS

- Get to know the members of other departments and form key relationships.

- Stay current with evidence-based practices affecting nursing and the healthcare environment.

- Consider becoming an expert in a chosen nursing specialty.

- Ask for help from others when you need it.

- Always understand the *what* and *why* of nursing work.

- Keep leaders informed of what you need in order to accomplish your nursing work.

DISCIPLINARY SILOS

Silos in patient care areas can exist when nurses perform certain functions and tasks, nursing assistants perform other specific tasks, and other clinical disciplines perform only the tasks appropriate for their specialty. This personal or professional task-oriented mindset can cause disjointed patient care. Although limits relative to each care provider's scope of practice may affect who is capable or allowed to perform specific tasks related to care provision, siloed work without communication is of no benefit to the team or the patient.

Disciplinary silos can cause confusion or a lack of clarity, sending a distinct message to the patient and family. The message might be misinterpreted as non-communicative specialists who only speak with each other through written word (in the medical record). This approach might unfortunately leave a patient or family member as the link to ensure each provider knows what the other provider is doing. A lack of communication and teamwork, either perceived or real, can cause a great deal of duplication (non–value added work) and frustration for each individual involved. Patients tire quickly when repetitively answering the same questions for each discipline, and families lose trust when nursing information does not coincide with directives provided by the medical provider.

Nurses burn out quickly when working in an environment that results from a lack of trust, no involvement in decision-making, and a lack of inclusion. Positive team behavior and optimal communication are necessary to create trust. Teams that communicate effectively are able to be proactive; thus, they handle issues before they arise and answer questions before they are asked. This can eliminate patient and family feelings of confusion.

Prepared caregivers can deliver care that appears seamless. Proactive teamwork creates excellence. Jennings (2008) identified that communication among nurses, both at the peer level and with leaders, decreases the amount of stress and burnout in nursing.

PRACTICE PEARLS

- Communication is the most influential way to eliminate silos in healthcare.
- Be honest in all communication for effective collaboration.
- Speak positively to build successful relationships with others or "manage up" teammates.
- Be a good example—be the teammate you want your co-workers to be.

ORGANIZATIONAL SILOS

Many of today's healthcare organizations have reorganized into larger systems due to the number of complex regulatory changes in the healthcare environment. Multi-hospital systems within a network have become more common. Some of the affiliations are formal, while others are not. However, new challenges have surfaced between sites or within the same system, especially when caregivers do not manage patients the same way. Examples include variable documentation systems, not using common systems in a uniform way, not planning care based on the most recent evidence, and not defining standardized policies and procedures.

Nurses working in system hospitals that do not work as effectively as they could or should can become frustrated with variances in procedures and practices that may not match the system policy to which they are held accountable. System policies typically represent the largest or most vocal hospital in the system but often neglect to review the application of the policy to each hospital in the system. This specifically can affect smaller organizations with fewer resources.

Litigation concerns and risk are often higher with such discrepancies because it appears a nurse simply did not follow policy. Although this may have been unintentional, it can create a great deal of stress for a nurse and his or her employer and can affect the nurse's future practice. Being involved in any type of legal situation is stressful and can cause a nurse to rethink his or her career choice. This may diminish a nurse's passion for the profession, resulting in tiring and fatigue. If there is no intervention, the symptoms may progress. This kind of burnout is a result of system or process challenges that affect individual care providers and their ability to perform their jobs.

Healthcare organizations, as well as patients, experience silos in nearly every healthcare encounter. Many of the pay-for-performance initiatives and governmental payment structures have caused healthcare facilities to rethink how they provide care in an effort to achieve a higher percentage of reimbursement per patient. This new system, while altruistic in theory to improve coordination and care, may have the opposite effect.

As value-based purchasing dictates program objectives and payments such as meaningful use and community assessments, organizations must become fluent in the new language. Nurses do not have a common knowledge about these structures and how they might affect their employer's bottom line. Historically, nursing has not been held accountable for practice outcomes in a financially focused arena. While quality has always been important to both nurses and patients from an outcome perspective, it is even more so today. These government programs also have the ability to levy financial penalties and taxes, which provide a new layer of heightened awareness and associated compliance.

If facilities do not comply with healthcare's rules and regulations as directed, they must develop plans of correction to achieve measurable metrics and do so within their budgetary constraints. The information also may become public. Although each of these functions alone can create positive outcomes for an organization and its patient population, they can also cause conflict. Nursing is changing. What it takes to be a nurse today is quite different than in previous times. This rapid-fire change in practice(s) is particularly complicated by the four generations of nurses in the workforce together.

In addition, the care continuum for patients has been widened with a new focus on what happens outside of an acute episodic hospital admission. Organizations must develop systems to track efforts to keep patients out of the hospital and thus, healthier. Hospitals have been forced to work closely with not only physicians and their clinics but also extended care facilities, skilled nursing facilities, rehabilitation facilities, and hospice organizations. Healthcare in general is drastically changing. This requires the removal of silos toward a new dawn of transparency.

An opening is necessary in the historically built walls of communication in order to succeed in the different, fiercely competitive healthcare market.

DEPARTMENTAL AND INTERLINKING SILOS

One example of how silos are interlinked and related to a clinical improvement project can be found in one hospital's efforts to decrease catheter-associated urinary tract infections.

Case 1: A team of nurses began by breaking down each step in the process for urinary catheter insertion, maintenance, and removal. The nurses also searched for best practices and relevant evidence in the literature. Based on the variety of sources of information, they made a plan for improvement. To implement the newly defined standards, the nurses began performing a peer-review process to assess competency of insertion and audits for compliance of the new maintenance requirements. During the project's implementation process, the nurses realized that nursing students rotating through their organizational departments were being taught to insert urinary catheters in a way that differed from what the hospital had deemed to be best practice. This variation did not meet the new competency requirement. Because the school was associated with the hospital, there was an easy avenue with which to address the variation in practice. Had it not been addressed, the variation could have caused a great deal of stress and frustration to both practicing and newly hired nurses as they took the time to isolate the cause of the variation.

Schools of nursing are another example of an interlinking silo that can produce conflict and variation in practice. Departments often have differing practices versus a single nursing standard. This is why it is important for clinical site instructors to know the current standards of nursing practice, as well as organizational and departmental policy for the facilities where their students are typically deployed.

EXTERNAL INFORMATION SILOS

Silos of information exist in the electronic information world, as well as in the physical world. One example is in pharmacies across the country. Pharmacies have experienced significant challenges in identifying practitioner diversion, inappropriate use of controlled substances, and medication reconciliation. Concerned parties include distributors, the Drug Enforcement Administration (DEA), Automation of Reports and Consolidated Orders System (ARCOS), as well as individual and corporately organized pharmacies.

Historically, each pharmacy and medical provider has been a silo. Typically, there was little communication and a lack of tracking information (Traynor, 2012). It was possible for medical providers to write prescriptions for the same patient, who might use several different pharmacies. There was no overlap or methodology to track duplication and drug usage or misuse.

Until the U.S. government began seeking the assessment of criminal activity relative to narcotic abuse, pharmacies had no reason to follow the throughput of medications or track the process for distribution. This enabled those seeking to abuse the system, such as drug abusers and drug dealers, to devise intricate schemes to profit from the loopholes. Eliminating the silos of communication in the pharmacy arena has significantly reduced the downstream problems of abuse often seen in emergency departments and provider offices.

Now, patients who choose to abuse healthcare systems are more easily identifiable. This has been a long-standing frustration for practicing medical providers and nurses. This type of encounter with patients significantly contributes to negative thinking and nursing burnout. The mental health system and the amount of drug abuse in the United States is a complex social and health problem.

116

Healthcare system abuse by patients who take no responsibility for their own health causes nurses to feel stressed. Nurses want to help others; however, this type of patient is difficult for a nurse to provide any intervention that is going to improve the outcome of the patient's health or the patient's ability to manage illness as independently as possible. The frustration can be exhausting. It is a challenge for nurses to feel any sense of accomplishment with care provided to this patient population.

The Maslach Burnout Inventory (MBI) is a tool that has been used in healthcare to measure burnout in nurses. The elements identified as important and contributory to the symptoms of burnout are emotional exhaustion, depersonalization, and decreased personal accomplishment (Vahey, Aiken, Sloane, Clarke, & Vargas, 2004). The survey has a number of associated items specific to measure three general scales with aspects of burnout relative to emotional exhaustion, depersonalization, and decreased personal accomplishment (StatisticsSolutions, 2015). Information about the MBI instrument can be found at https://prezi.com/bn2vlq3fjzj8/maslach-burnout-inventory-3rd-edition.

PRACTICE PEARLS

- Seek satisfying work.
- Excellent communication keeps patients and caregivers safe.
- Do your part to eliminate silos.

CONFLICT: SURVIVAL OF THE FITTEST

Nursing and other clinical disciplines' task lists are getting longer. The amount of work to be done can easily cause nurses to feel overwhelmed.

Solo thinking, such as a "survival of the fittest" mentality, drives people to behave in a competitive manner rather than working as a team. This type of thinking and isolationist approach to practice creates a spirit of "dog eat dog," also known as "nurses eating their young" (Cole & Cole, 2005, p. 43). Cole and Cole (2005) reported that training related to teamwork does little to no good when the organization's culture is not supportive. Cultures that support behaving in a positive manner embrace effective communication and transparency. Frequently, this journey begins with a dynamic nurse leader at the helm in the organization and spreads, one nurse at a time.

Unintentional silos of information have become the norm in healthcare. Systems are not interfaced, software changes, data is not presented in a useful way to be used as information, and so on. When conflict exists in the workplace, often those involved are looking for someone to blame versus providing an effective solution to the problem. This knee-jerk reaction to hoard information gives power to the party who has it and diminishes the effectiveness of those who do not have access. It's not terribly uncommon to hear a nurse say, "He should do his own work," or, "If she were here, she would know the patient went to radiology," or, "That is not my patient."

Nurses and units that do not work well together put patients at risk. An unhealthy environment of care leaves nurses feeling alone, angry, frustrated, and ultimately unsatisfied with their work, the environment, and the leadership. This can compromise both the patient's experience and the care provided. As frustrating and stress-invoking as inter- and intradepartmental conflict can be, conflict can have an even larger facility impact related to regulatory compliance.

Case 2: One hospital example includes a well-meaning quality/survey-readiness nurse who forwarded all types of survey-related information on to the leadership. She neglected to filter the information or provide any explanation of applicability for their assigned areas of responsibility. Although her efforts to keep the leaders informed (to ultimately achieve a successful survey result) were not malicious, she inadvertently angered many of the departmental leaders. The leaders had one expectation of an interpretation of the regulations and the quality nurse had another of providing the information, with an assumption that no translation was needed. The leaders felt they did not have time to sort through the mass of forwarded email or to read all of the information. In addition, the survey-readiness nurse was frustrated because the leaders never responded to her messages, and she felt they were ignoring her attempts to provide them the information they needed to be successful. In this case, conflict was caused by differing expectations, where communication was not clear and feedback was not offered in a proactive manner.

This example raises a number of questions: Was the quality nurse a fit for the position? Were her job expectations clear? Was she provided the appropriate training? Did she receive performance feedback on a regular basis? Unfortunately, this story ends in a negative outcome for the nurse because no one ever approached her about her style of communication. She merely lost her position in quality as a survey coordinator and was given an alternate assignment. What kind of precedent did this set? Unfortunately, it caused a higher level of mistrust and inter-facility conflict. The employees viewed the leadership as unable to fix a simple problem with communication.

Stress, fatigue, and burnout can be created by silos, the work environment, organizational culture, suboptimal work processes, and position fit. Symptoms of dissatisfaction are evident with nurses who move from position to position. They are usually searching for something. Could the cycle be broken if instead they received honest performance feedback? Could the situation be improved by good leadership? A multitude of nurses stay in organizations that function as "secret societies" because they believe they can make a difference, are loyal employees, and believe the organization needs them. These organizations are fortunate because nurses are an invaluable resource for effective organizational performance. Decreasing stress, fatigue, and the potential for burnout in the work environment would inevitably decrease risk for a host of negative outcomes.

COMPETITION FOR LIMITED RESOURCES

Budgetary constraints in healthcare organizations result in limited resources. Every healthcare organization across the care continuum is attempting to work with fewer available resources. Capital expenditures have been difficult to secure, and the bottom line is that this affects infrastructure. Where organizations most often tend to fail is in an honest assessment of the departmental needs throughout the organization. The competition for resources is fierce, and the money generally goes to new products, services, and buildings versus items in the infrastructure to provide daily patient care. Often the most vocal or even the most revenue-generating departments are the ones selected to receive the majority of capital budget items.

Not having the appropriate equipment or supplies for nurses to carry out their duties can be maddening. Precious time is often wasted looking for necessary items to complete care delivery. Because many items can be purchased at a discount in bulk, it makes sense to stock inventory at an organizational versus departmental level. Nurses have a responsibility to participate in designing effective systems for placement and replacement of capital and disposable items. Standardization of equipment and supply is not just good business but facilitates movement of nursing staff among and between units. Standardization improves patient safety and care delivery. Nurses should be familiar with equipment and the environment and should have the necessary supplies and tools to safely perform their jobs.

PRACTICE PEARL

Tools + Talent = Success

PERSONNEL SHORTAGES

With ever-increasing challenges for healthcare entities to perform, staffing often becomes a target. Labor is the most costly expense in nearly all organizations. In recent decades, securing the correct type of staff by skill and experience has become more challenging. In addition, staffing ratios between nurses and patients have changed. Commonly, more assigned patients and less nursing staff has been the result. Some states have even legislated ratios and/or mandated staffing committees with smaller numbers of patients per nurse. Sadly, the ratio limits have not produced the clinical care outcomes as predicted. The good news is that when labor expectations are made clear, whether with ratios, committees, or joint leadership, the goals or targets to predict financial outcomes are understood by all.

The upshots of personnel shortages are concerns about recruitment and retention; patient safety; and sicker hospitalized patients requiring more skilled and qualified clinical staff. Projections for future demand of healthcare and the mismatch of projected clinically trained resources is daunting. Additionally, nursing leaders express concern about nurses' training and bedside nurses being too task-focused, with little ability for critical thinking. Although this may be true, the preface for this concerning change in nursing performance is most likely due to the ever-increasing task list. Nurses have to give medications, educate patients about them, and follow up on their effectiveness. Nurses perform daily patient hygiene, ambulation, bathroom assistance, and assessments, and provide physician support. Nurses often find themselves merely surviving the day instead of thriving in their role as nurse and lead communicator in the patient-healing process.

It is doubtful anything substantive will be done in the near future about the variability in nurse staffing and ratios. Cost is a driving factor; therefore, nurses must learn how to utilize the available resources to provide the best care. In studies conducted in nearly 125 Veteran Administration (VA) facilities, the dual benefit of efficiency and teamwork for healthcare disciplines led to greater patient satisfaction (Meterko, Mohr, & Young, 2004). Culture affects outcomes. In a separate Taiwanese study by Chang, Ma, Chiu, Lin, and Lee (2009), a similar result was found. If a healthcare organization can create a culture of teamwork, it is likely to have higher levels of job and customer satisfaction. Patients expect to be cared for by a team of attentive people working together to ensure healing.

Emerging roles in nursing, such as nursing informaticists, have become popular across the country. As organizations move to an electronic health or medical record, integrated records of various types of encounters are improving communication for providers and patients. Nursing has always held a vital role in communication. Nurses are often the coordinators of care who facilitate communication between the various disciplines. This is necessary to achieve highly reliable and safe care for the best patient outcomes. Effective communication decreases stress for both patients and providers. While the electronic medical or health record is not designed to replace communication between healthcare providers, it is a key indicator of the kind of communication existing in an organization (Herman, 2014).

THE PRESSURE TO PERFORM

The Affordable Care Act of 2010 has driven much of the recent change in the healthcare landscape. In 2014, the *Journal of Healthcare Management* published a study in which frontline staff were surveyed about why change in their organization was unsuccessful. The most common failure was poor implementation planning. Two other significant findings, in the top reasons for project failure, were ineffective communication (top-down) and little-to-no teamwork (Longnecker, Longnecker, & Gering, 2014).

Communication and teamwork have continually surfaced as key elements to organizational success. Is it really this simple? Could all silos be eliminated? One of the leadership lessons printed in the *Journal of Healthcare Management* (Longnecker et al., 2014) conveyed leaders must lead by example. When organizations segment disciplines within the leadership structure, care processes become fragmented. It is more difficult for frontline staff to connect all of the dots in the care continuum. It is challenging to understand each care provider's role and subsequent limitations. Nurses must learn how best to integrate ancillary peers into the cycle of work. The design of the organizational structure is crucial to eliminate silos and facilitate communication.

Cassady's lecture in 2013 described how teamwork, as a core element, is essential to the provision of better healthcare. Cassady (2013) also recommended teamwork be infused in each discipline's educational development to benefit communication. Cassady cited Patrick Lencioni's groundbreaking work showcased in the book, *The Five Dysfunctions of a Team*. A summary and visual model of Lencioni's work is displayed in Figure 6.2.

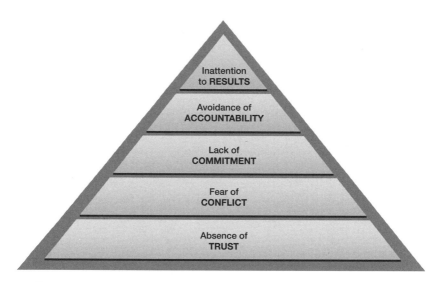

Figure 6.2   The five dysfunctions of a team. Copyright © Patrick Lencioni, 2002. Used with permission.

Creative organizations have been able to take teamwork beyond theory. Application is evident in organizational process, policy, and procedure.

Case 3: For example, Baptist Health in Arkansas designed a care model using every distinct discipline in the healthcare organization. The model was designed to screen every incoming patient for necessary consults, regardless of discipline, based on patient needs. An example of a non-clinical discipline in the model included information technology personnel, who were instrumental in assisting clinicians with the practicalities of documentation in the electronic health record. This unique team approach led to higher levels of trust among the disciplines. The model also allowed the admitting nurse to design and appropriate specific care teams based on individual and unique patient needs.

As the disciplines worked to refine the model, communication improved, duplication decreased, and teamwork was enhanced. The team also learned that when frontline disciplines are included in the process, they have a better understanding of objectives and learn the organization's methods to reach its goals. Buy-in was better obtained for organizational resource alignment. Strong healthcare systems communicate clearly and share results openly (Cassady, 2013).

PRACTICE PEARLS

- Buy-in is obtained though clear communication.
- When nurses are included in decision-making, they commit wholeheartedly to the outcome.
- Nurses who participate in shared governance lead others.
- Be a valuable participant in problem-solving.

"Inter-professional collaborative practice happens when multiple health workers from different professional backgrounds work together with patients, families, caregivers, and communities to deliver the highest quality of care" (Gittell, Godfrey, & Thistlethwaite, 2013, p. 210). Anytime organizations build collaborative team care models or practice patient-centered care, they are engaging in inter-professional collaborative practice. The researchers further defined relational coordination as a mutually reinforcing process of communicating and relating for the purpose of task integration. The call for organizations to implode and rebuild organizational design, structure, and functions in new cross-functional, team-focused work environments is now.

Consideration should be given to rebuilding every department and every process, from hiring to the management of conflict resolution. Concepts such as shared governance, interdisciplinary care models, and town hall meetings are great methods of sharing information for improved communication:

- Shared governance is a model of professional practice founded on partnership among leaders and staff. Shared governance promotes collaborative efforts that lead to shared decisions, responsibility, accountability, quality, and safety (Porter-O'Grady, 1991). The promotion of shared governance includes interdisciplinary care models—inclusive versus exclusive groups of varied care providers.

- Town hall meetings are an incredibly effective way to get in front of your team and ensure they are heard. The concept of town hall meetings is most likely taken from the political arena. Town hall meetings are used in a variety of formal organizations such as unions, campaigns, and groups such as the national nursing action coalition. Town hall meetings provide clear direction about the objective of the group, session, or meeting and allow opportunity for statements and questions from those present.

One strategy is when a healthcare organization has a big announcement and wants to ensure the employees understand it, it can hold a town hall meeting to offer information, hear concerns, and most importantly, ensure everyone understands the objective and is focused and committed to working toward the same goal.

CONCLUSION

We can no longer operate "business as usual" in the healthcare systems of today that have evolved over time. They are just too stressful—for patients and providers. Healthcare must undergo radical change encompassing the patient experience and innovative strategies to provide better care. Nurses must lead by recognizing the value in becoming an active participant in the team and using their collective voice to drive needed changes in care delivery models and practice.

Healthcare entities must become the kind of organizations that breed healthy work cultures by breaking apart silos, encouraging free-flowing communication, and providing safe care with highly reliable outcomes. Thus, a decrease in stress and fatigue in healthcare work environments should result. The potential for the internal strain of silos to cause burnout for nurses and others who choose a career in healthcare should be banished for a better future. The next chapter investigates how the healthcare culture can exacerbate stress and burnout.

REFERENCES

Cassady, S. (2013). *The Linda Crane lecture:* From silos to bridges: Preparing effective teams for a better delivery system. *Cardiopulmonary Physical Therapy Journal, 24*(2), 5–11.

Chang, W. Y., Ma, J. C., Chiu, H. T., Lin, K. C., & Lee, P. H. (2009). Job satisfaction and perceptions of quality of patient care, collaboration, and teamwork in acute care hospitals. *Journal of Advanced Nursing, 65*(9), 1946–1955. doi: 10.1111/j.1365-2648.2009.05085.x

Cole, L., & Cole, M. (2005). The teamwork values statement. In Cole & Cole (Eds.), *People smart leaders* (p. 43). Winchester, VA: Oakhill Press.

Gittell, J. H., Godfrey, M., & Thistlethwaite, J. (2013). Interprofessional collaborative practice and relational coordination: Improving healthcare through relationships. *Journal of Interprofessional Care, 27*(3) 210–213. doi: 10.3109/13561820.2012.730564

Herman, B. (2014). Nurses take bigger role in health IT. *Modern Healthcare, 44*(45), 32–36.

Jennings, B. (2008). Work stress and burnout among nurses: Role of the work environment and working conditions. In R. G. Hughes, *Patient safety and quality: An evidence-based handbook for nurses* (Chapter 26, pp. 4/22). Rockville, MD: Agency for Healthcare Research and Quality.

Lencioni, P. (2002). *The five dysfunctions of a team: A leadership fable.* San Francisco, CA: Jossey-Bass.

Longnecker, C. O., Longnecker, P. D., & Gering, J. T. (2014). Why hospital improvement efforts fail: A view from the front line. *Journal of Healthcare Management, 59*(2), 148–157.

Meterko, M., Mohr, D. C., & Young, G. Y. (2004). Teamwork culture and patient satisfaction in hospitals. *Medical Care, 42*(5), 492–498.

Porter-O'Grady, T. (1991). Shared governance for nursing: Part 1: Creating the new organization. *AORN Journal, 53*:2.

silo. (n.d.). In *Merriam-Webster's online dictionary.* Retrieved from www.merriam-webster.com/dictionary/silo

StatisticsSolutions. (2015). *Maslach burnout inventory.* Retrieved from http://www.statisticssolutions.com/maslach-burnout-inventory-mbi/

Traynor, K. (2012). Data silos impede progress against prescription drug abuse. *American Journal of Health System Pharmacy, 69,* 628–632.

Tucker, A. L. (2009). Workarounds and resiliency on the front lines of health care. *Perspective, AHRQ, Web M&M.* Retrieved from http://webmm.ahrq.gov/perspective.aspx?perspectiveID=78

Tuckman, B. W., & Jensen, M. A. (1977). Stages in small group development revisited. *Group and Organisation Studies, 2,* 419–427.

Tuckman, B.W. (1965). Development in small groups. *Psychological Bulletin, 63,* 384–399.

Tuckman, B. (1965). *Four (five) stages of team development.* Retrieved from https://www.mindtools.com/pages/article/newLDR_86.htm

7

THE SOCIAL MILIEU (CULTURE)

Rita Haxton, DNP, RN, NEA-BC

OBJECTIVES

- Understand the importance of culture.

- Build a positive work environment.

- Understand the value of relationships in getting your job done.

- Explore how being engaged affects your satisfaction at work.

- Consider how nurses can lead the charge in creating patient-centered care models.

As nurses, we dream of finding the perfect job where we can care for the patients that give us the most professional satisfaction. If you are a person who loves a critical challenge and an adrenaline rush, you may want to work in an emergency department or a critical care unit. If you like having the ability to make long-term connections with patients, you may choose home care, a dialysis unit, or long-term care. One of the best reasons to choose nursing is the diversity in the profession and the multiple opportunities nurses have of where they can work. Aside from the reasons you might have chosen to become a nurse, one factor that may significantly influence an employee's feelings about work is the work environment.

THE IMPORTANCE OF A POSITIVE WORK ENVIRONMENT

The work environment has a major impact on an employee's job satisfaction. *Work environment* involves everything that is a part of the employee's work, such as his or her relationships with co-workers and department leaders, the organizational culture, and access to professional development activities. Taking into account commuting time, hours at work, and the time we spend thinking and worrying about our jobs, we spend more waking hours at work than we do at home or in life's other activities. The power of a positive work environment cannot be underestimated. The impact it can have about how people think about work and their resulting happiness with work is immense. The opposite, a negative work environment, has the potential to increase stress for nurses and cause burnout.

In 2001, the American Association of Critical-Care Nurses (AACN) was one of the first professional nursing organizations to make a commitment to actively promote the development of healthy work environment standards. The decision to develop these standards sprang from the organization's dedication to optimal patient care and the desire to promote an environment that supports excellence in nursing practice for acute and critical care nurses. Read about the association's most up-to-date work at http://www.aacn.org/wd/hwe/content/hwehome. pcms?menu=hwe.

The AACN standards for establishing and sustaining healthy work environments include (AACN, 2005):

- **Skilled communication.** Nurses must be as proficient in communication skills as they are in clinical skills.

    1. Be honest and transparent.

    2. Don't spread gossip.

    3. Be prepared to discuss a patient by utilizing a mnemonic such as Situation-Background-Assessment-Recommendations (SBAR). More information about SBAR can be found at http://www.saferhealthcare.com/sbar/what-is-sbar/.

    4. Support new nurses and model good communication skills to help them successfully transition to the practice environment.

- **True collaboration.** Nurses must be relentless in pursuing and fostering true collaboration.

  1. Focus on developing teamwork with colleagues.

  2. Utilize clear communication with peers and providers for patient safety.

- **Effective decision-making.** Nurses must be valued and committed partners in making policy, directing and evaluating clinical care, and leading organizational operations.

  1. Get involved in unit operations (unit councils).

  2. When a practice issue is identified, research best practices and make recommendations for change.

- **Appropriate staffing.** Staffing must ensure an effective match between patient needs and nurse competencies.

  1. Support staffing by acuity or complexity of patient care needs.

  2. Work together (as a team) to support patient-care requirements during times of staff shortages.

- **Meaningful recognition.** Nurses must be recognized and must recognize others for the value each brings to the work of the organization.

  1. Recognize fellow nurses who do a good job.

  2. Distinguish other team members (who are not nurses) who support great patient care.

- **Authentic leadership.** Nurse leaders must fully embrace the imperative of a healthy work environment, authentically live it, and engage others in its achievement.

  1. Be a role model. Leaders must demonstrate transformational leadership skills to achieve the best results.

  2. Help others take action by offering the ability to influence decisions about departmental processes.

  3. Look for signs of increased stress levels and use available organizational and professional resources to mitigate them.

DEVELOPING A POSITIVE WORK ENVIRONMENT

A positive work environment can only develop with support from leadership and employees who work together. Rosenberg (2008) discussed how a leader can affect the culture and how the culture of an organization affects a new leader joining an organization. In addition, Rosenberg (2008) concluded that the entire purpose of leadership is to create a culture.

Leaders can develop the structure and a strong base for a positive work environment. The importance of each person's role in creating a positive work environment should not be underestimated. Benefits of a healthy work culture are evident when the focus is on patient safety, teamwork, and the delivery of quality care.

How do employees and leaders work together to create a positive work environment? Is it possible to harness the positive energy from each person's perspective? Rosenberg (2008) identified similar qualities as those in more recent writings such as Poh's work in 2014. The talents necessary for a positive work environment require each person to exhibit the following:

- *Communication*
  - Open communication addresses the need to be heard, feel valued, and want to belong in an organization.
  - Understanding the organizational mission, philosophy, and values clarifies the purpose of work.
  - Good two-way communication encourages the sharing of ideas for improvement.

- *Work-life balance*
  - Recognize the potential for imbalance between work and life's priorities.
  - Active management strategies will reduce stress, fatigue, and the potential for burnout, thus improving job-related satisfaction.

- *Professional development*
  - Nursing requires lifelong learning.
  - Strong professional development activities should be available, and nurses should take advantage of the opportunities.
  - Equal priority should be placed on enhancing clinical expertise and interpersonal skills.

- *Recognition*

  - Recognize peers by saying "thank you."

  - Look for what is going right in the work environment and reinforce positive behavior.

- *Strong team spirit*

  - Teamwork is critical in healthcare. Patients receive the best care when each team member brings a high level of expertise and performance.

  - Team challenges facilitate learning. Common goals bring those with different perspectives and styles together.

Finding ways to blend these five important criteria can create a positive work environment. Nurses and other staff will enjoy coming to work. Teamwork will be evident. Organizations that support professional development foster and encourage the growth of professional nurses. Feelings of challenge, value, pride, professional competence, and confidence to solve complex problems will result. The most important improvements in the culture will be safe systems, a positive team, and good patient outcomes.

PRACTICE PEARLS

- Walk the talk. People observe others and choose how to behave based on what is acceptable in the culture.

- Rewards and recognition must be consistent with organizational values.

- Become passionate about your work. Enthusiasm is contagious. People like to be around positive people and a part of success.

- Get "networked" for the best information sharing in the organization. The more people you know, the easier it is to get things done.

- Communicate clearly and honestly. Be straightforward.

HUMAN CAPITAL AND THE VALUE OF RELATIONSHIPS

The greatest asset in any healthcare organization is the people. No technology can replace the human touch in nursing and healthcare. Whom to hire is one of the most important choices a leader will make because it affects multiple aspects of any organization. Many organizational leaders say employees are their greatest assets, but their actions are inconsistent with their words. It's disingenuous to say this if too few resources are chronically allocated for professional development, staffing is always too lean, vacancy rates are always too high, and so on.

Because nurses are the largest workforce in healthcare, they have an opportunity to mold the future. Nurses can help create work environments where employees feel valued. Nurses can and should be considered front-line leaders. Nurses can be organizational ambassadors just as they are patient advocates. Exit interviews show that most people don't choose to leave an organization because of the executives. They choose to leave because of their peers' behavior, the work environment, or the relationship with their direct supervisor (or lack thereof). As an employee, nurses can make a difference by working with leaders to develop an environment where everyone feels valued.

One of the questions asked in almost every employee satisfaction or employee engagement survey is, "Do you have a best friend at work?" Most people wonder what that has to do with anything related to the work environment and don't believe it is important to have a best friend at work. However, it is important to be able to trust the people you work with. Trust facilitates the development of friendships. Friends are loyal, supportive, and can be counted on for help in times of need. In order to develop close friendships, you have to be willing to share some of the intimate details of your life in confidence. People are more likely to leave a job when they do not have positive and strong relationships with their co-workers or departmental leaders.

SHARP HEALTHCARE

In healthcare, there are some great examples of companies doing the right things. For example, Sharp HealthCare, based in San Diego, California, clearly values its human capital. Its healthcare system includes four acute care hospitals, three specialty hospitals, a number of medical groups, and its own health plan. This includes over 14,000 employees and 2,600 affiliated physicians. The organization made a decision in 2001 to dedicate itself to transforming the healthcare experience. Understanding the value of human capital, it started this movement with its employees.

The overall vision at Sharp was to:

> "Become the best place for employees to work, the best place for physicians to practice medicine, the best place for patients to receive care, and ultimately the best healthcare system in the universe." (Sharp, n.d., p. 4)

The model developed by Sharp HealthCare has three core components (Adamson, 2009, p. 22):

- Experience and performance improvement designed to actively engage team members, at all levels, in creating positive change related to the workplace experience and the customer experience.

- Accountability systems and structures ensuring alignment of goals across the organization.

- Learning and development that launched the Sharp University, a corporate university designed to provide education and development for leaders, team members, and affiliated physicians.

The results at Sharp HealthCare, secondary to its focus on employees, have demonstrated the value of employee engagement. Since the transformation began, the results have been astounding. One of the most important lessons to be learned from this example of transformation is that the higher employee engagement, the more positive improvement you'll enjoy. Sharp has engaged its workforce to reduce employee turnover, achieve higher patient and employee satisfaction, garner annual improvement in quality metrics, and improve market share and net revenue for the organization (Adamson & Rhodes, 2009).

In 2007, Sharp HealthCare received the Malcolm Baldrige National Quality Award for organizational excellence (Adamson, 2009). It's one of the most prestigious awards an organization can receive. The Malcolm Baldrige criteria provide a prized framework for measuring performance and planning in an uncertain environment. The structure is perfect for the healthcare environment, where there is controlled chaos and an uncertain environment.

The Baldrige criteria can help any healthcare organization achieve and sustain the highest national levels of patient safety and loyalty; health outcomes in the areas of acute myocardial infarction, heart failure, pneumonia, and other conditions; physician and staff satisfaction or engagement, with a focus on registered nurses; revenue and market share; and community service (National Institute of Standards and Technology [NIST], 2010).

As this story illustrates, having a happy and engaged workforce has a positive impact on productivity and morale, reduces employee stress, and improves employee retention. So what can a nurse do to become an engaged employee who finds happiness and joy in his or her work? The decision to find happiness and joy rests with each individual.

FINDING HAPPINESS AT WORK

Optimistic, hopeful, and happy staff members can convey those attributes to patients and other staff through developed relationships in the workplace. There are work environments just the opposite where patients and co-workers are cranky, pessimistic, and depressed. The impact of attitude and effort always comes back to you. Aren't you drawn to people who laugh, have hope, and care about others? Aren't you happier around patients who are involved in their own recovery, who exhibit hope and optimism, and who make you laugh? This is most likely the most valuable lesson in relationships—it begins with you.

Dr. Martin Seligman is recognized as the father of the theory of positive psychology. Seligman spent the majority of his career studying depression and learned helplessness. However, after a number of years in practice, he changed his thinking. In 2002, he published a book about happiness titled *Authentic Happiness*. In the theory of authentic happiness, he included three elements: positive emotion, engagement, and meaning.

After development of his original authentic happiness theory, he received input from his students and fellow psychologists over the next 10 years. Seligman then expanded it and changed it to the Well-Being Theory. The new theory added two elements to the previous three elements for a new total of five critical elements thought to achieve happiness and the ability to flourish. The revised theory of well-being includes these areas of measurement, which he terms "PERMA" (Seligman, 2011):

- **P**ositive emotion (which includes happiness and life satisfaction)
- **E**ngagement
- **R**elationships
- **M**eaning and purpose
- **A**ccomplishment

The goal of positive psychology (in authentic happiness) is to increase the amount of happiness in your own life and in the world. The Well-Being Theory posits a slightly different goal of expanding or increasing the amount of flourishing in your life and in the world (Seligman, 2011). Flourishing speaks to the quality of your life and the impact you have over your individual circumstances.

Morale is simply the collective happiness of the workforce. The workforce is comprised of individuals who can each decide to have a positive or negative effect on the whole. The success of any office, department, or service provider is dependent on the individual investment of people in how they think, how they act, and what they do. There is no success unless people make it happen.

It is often easier to think negatively and want to blame others for the current circumstances. However, much of the difficulty in life is a result of the atmosphere and who is in it. What is most difficult is realizing that you have the power to change your thinking and subsequent actions. The secret to happiness, success, satisfaction, and fulfillment is not doing what you like but liking what you do. This includes liking the surroundings, the people, and the work.

Being happy all the time is an unrealistic expectation. Happiness comes with learning the skills of living in the present, valuing each moment, and making the best of each situation. Certain experiences, job tasks, and people might make it easier to be happy. However, they do not have the power to influence your ability to be happy or unhappy.

ENGAGEMENT FOR SATISFACTION (PERSONAL AND CUSTOMER)

Since 2000, the Gallup organization has been tracking employee engagement. The year 2014 marked the lowest employee engagement reading. Gallup noted that the number of workers who were actively engaged in their job was less than one-third, at 31.5% (Adkins, 2015). Over 50% of employees were not engaged; they appeared to have no passion for their work and were "just putting in time." The remaining 18% of employees were thought to be actively disengaged. Unfortunately, the disengaged group of employees usually demonstrated their unhappiness in an active fashion to other employees and undermined the work of the engaged employees.

The value of an engaged workforce has been shown to directly affect the success of an organization. The competence and skills of these employees are reflected in enthusiasm, motivation, and loyalty to an organization. It has a major impact on the overall culture of the organization and the level of customer service provided by the organization. The spirit of teamwork, organizational support, living the stated mission and vision, as well as adherence to standards are critical to productivity, innovation, and the ability to create an exceptional patient experience.

One of the most well-known and earliest adopters of using an engaged workforce to drive organizational improvement and show the difference it can make was Quint Studer at Baptist Health Care in Pensacola, Florida. The impact to customer satisfaction was amazing; the hospital virtually went from the bottom to the top. Studer developed his method, formed his own company, and has since helped hundreds of hospitals implement evidence-based leadership systems. These leadership systems have helped organizations attain and sustain outstanding results in improved organizational performance and patient-care outcomes. In 2010, the Studer Group won the Malcolm Baldrige Award. In addition, the Studer Group has coached 10 of the 18 Malcolm Baldrige Award recipients.

PRACTICE PEARLS

Determining whether you're an engaged and happy employee requires self-reflection about your state of being. Here are a few important questions to ask yourself:

- What things do I do at work that might be perceived as negative?
- What physical or verbal attitudes might be perceived as negative?
- What puts me in a bad mood at work? How do I contribute?
- What puts me in a good mood at work? How do I contribute?
- Do I make a difference at work?

Awareness and self-reflection are the first steps toward making change. Improvement and a path of self-discovery can be rewarding. Making a conscious decision to influence your own happiness and joy in your work can yield other collateral benefits. It may include improved relationships both at and outside of work, a sense of calm, and feelings of less stress.

Taking responsibility for negative feelings about work and changing your thinking or reaction to the negativity can provide relief from stress and fatigue and can lessen the potential to reach burnout. How a person perceives a given situation is a predictor of subsequent action, not necessarily an appropriate assessment of the situation itself. Be careful of others' ability to influence your behavior through their negativity.

It is well known that customers who are satisfied will be passive but loyal advocates. Dissatisfied customers are known to be active complainants who will share their customer experiences with many others. Estimates of how many people become aware of negative perceptions or experiences are growing with access to social media and other online platforms to post their experiences.

Customer satisfaction has always been important to hospital and healthcare providers. This is a people business. An unsatisfied customer can have a negative impact on reputation and is more likely to consider legal recourse. The importance of scoring well has escalated for hospitals on the Hospital Consumer Assessment of Healthcare Providers and Systems (HCAHPS). The survey has received increased emphasis since the establishment of the Patient Protection and Affordable Care Act of 2010 (frequently called Obamacare).

The "pay for performance" payment scheme that resulted from this new law reduces the Medicare diagnosis-related group payments for all hospitals (Medicare.gov, n.d.). Savings are then redistributed at a later date according to individual hospital performance. The public can now search for quality data and hospital performance via the *Hospital Compare* website at https://www.medicare.gov/hospitalcompare/About/What-Is-HOS.html.

In the beginning, 70% of the Total Performance Score (TPS) was determined by Clinical Process of Care outcomes, and 30% was from Patient Experience of Care scoring. By 2015, the Total Performance Score (TPS) is now comprised of the Clinical Process of Care domain score (weighted as 20% of the TPS), the Patient Experience of Care domain (weighted as 30% of the TPS), the Outcome domain score (weighted as 30% of the TPS), and the Efficiency domain score (weighted as 20% of the TPS). Although measurement has shifted into other areas, patient experience still accounts for 30% of the possible negative or positive financial impact (Centers for Medicare & Medicaid Services [CMS], n.d.). You can read more about the intricacies of the Total Performance Score information at https://www.medicare.gov/hospitalcompare/data/total-performance-scores.html.

Read more about the entire pay for performance program written by Health Affairs at http://www.healthaffairs.org/healthpolicybriefs/brief.php?brief_id=78.

Nurses know they must be responsible to take care of sick or vulnerable patients. The need to improve patient experience scores often frustrates nurses. Organizational strategies are frequently viewed as superficial. Nurses are challenged with a number of systems beyond their direct control, which may present obstacles in providing care. Examples include cumbersome discharge processes, late provider rounding, physicians not communicating with patients and families, as well as complex family issues. Improving patient experience scores is a complex task. It can be very complicated in the inpatient hospital setting. Movement toward a patient-centric model, which focuses on patient needs and includes all members of the healthcare team, is a good place to start.

The Planetree Model for Patient Centered Care, created by patient Angelica Thieriot, was one of the first such patient-centric models created. Thieriot dreamed of what a hospital could be if a patient were treated like a whole person with his or her body, mind, and spirit being supported, and where the importance of caring, kindness, and respect were as important as technical skills (Frampton, 2009). The goal of the Planetree model was to change the hospital environment from a provider-centric one, which historically has been designed for the convenience of the practitioner, to an environment centered *around* the patient. It focused more on personalized care and promoted patient engagement in that care (Frampton, 2009).

> Today, Planetree, Inc. is a mission based not-for-profit organization that partners with healthcare organizations around the world and across the care continuum to transform how care is delivered. Powered by over 50,000 focus groups with patients, families, and staff, and over 35 years of experience working with healthcare organizations, Planetree is uniquely positioned to represent the patient voice and advance how professional caregivers engage with patients and families. Guided by a foundation in 10 components of patient centered care, Planetree informs policy at a national level, aligns strategies at a system level, guides implementation of care delivery practices at an organizational level, and facilitates compassionate human interactions at a deeply personal level. Our philosophical conviction that patient centered care is the "right thing to do" is supported by a structured process that enables sustainable change. (Planetree, 2014)

Thieriot described her original experience as follows:

- Sound medical care

- Institutional, impersonal, and alienating environment

- Bare white walls, excessive noise, nightly disturbances, and limited visitation

- Inadequate access to information related to her care and treatment

The first Planetree model unit opened in San Francisco on a 13-bed medical-surgical unit in 1985. Since then, the Planetree model members have continued to develop best practices to move organizations to a more patient-centered model of care. Planetree has identified 10 components of today's contemporary model:

- Human interaction
- Family, friends, and social support
- Access to information
- Healing environments through architectural design
- Food and nutrition
- Arts and entertainment
- Spirituality
- Human touch
- Complementary therapies
- Healthy communities

You can learn more about the Planetree model at http://planetree.org/.

THE NURSE'S ROLE IN PATIENT-CENTERED CARE

What is the nurse's role in moving the hospital to a more patient- and family-centered care environment? The nurse is often the one professional who spends the most time with patients. They are truly the patient advocates. They communicate, collaborate, and negotiate on behalf of patients. They help to translate concerns between multiple medical providers and patients. The nurse has an opportunity to provide care to the patient and family with compassion, the ability to focus on quality and patient safety during their interactions, and the ability to reduce patient anxiety about their care by providing education. Nurses can develop a trusting relationship with patients and family. Since 1999, Gallup's surveys have shown nursing as the profession with the highest rating for honesty and ethical standards (Riffkin, 2014). The only year that nurses did not have the top spot was 2001, after the 9/11 tragedy, and that year was awarded to firefighters.

Patient experience is always going to be a high concern for nurses. The nurse will likely be the person to establish the strongest relationship with a patient and his or her family. Many times the nurse will mediate misunderstandings, apologize for others' behavior or actions, and share the truth. Nurses need to take the lead in creating a healing environment. Healthcare leaders and organizations need to facilitate excellent patient experiences in a positive culture in all of the areas of healthcare.

CONCLUSION

The importance of culture and a positive work environment cannot be overstated in improving job satisfaction; it is critical for the retention of nurses both in organizations and in the profession of nursing. Every nurse, whether a staff nurse or a nurse leader, has the power to influence and impact the work environment in a positive or a negative way. Each individual has the ability to choose his or her level of engagement in the work environment.

After reflecting on the power of a positive work environment and the benefits of working with an engaged workforce, think about how you can begin to make a difference. The concepts detailed in *Random Kind-*

ness and Senseless Acts of Beauty, a children's book by Anne Herbert and M. Paloma Pavel (2014), outline the idea that we are all in the circle together. Each person can become an agent of goodness and beauty if her or she so chooses (Herbert & Pavel, 2014).

Senseless acts of beauty could be viewed as those things that are above and beyond the normal work expectations. It is not necessarily about doing more work, but doing work well. It is about showing unexpected appreciation and compassion to others. This could be as simple as writing a sincere note of praise, bringing food to share with co-workers, putting a flower in someone's mailbox, or making a decision to sincerely compliment five people during the day. The ideas are endless. People look forward to committing to and receiving senseless acts of beauty.

PRACTICE PEARL

Consider a senseless act of beauty campaign. It could lead to a new culture and bring the "beauty" back to nursing and healthcare.

So, how might the work environment be changed? The more engaged individuals are in their environment, the more likely they will be able to influence and impact decisions. The best outcomes occur when collaborative multidisciplinary teams interact. No nurse works alone in healthcare. Collectively, nurses can have a very powerful voice, and they hold one of the most important healthcare team roles—that of patient advocate. Their ability to influence others can lead change in creating better patient-centered models of care for the future. The next chapter takes a look at the clout of allies and why relationship-building in healthcare is crucial.

REFERENCES

Adamson, G., & Rhodes, S. (2009). *The complete guide to transforming the patient experience.* Marblehead, MA: HcPro.

Adkins, A. (2015, January 28). Majority of U.S. employees not engaged despite gains in 2014. *Gallup.* Retrieved from http://www.gallup.com/poll/181289/majority-employees-not-engaged-despite-gains-2014.aspx

American Association of Critical-Care Nurses (AACN). (2005). *AACN's standards for establishing and sustaining a healthy work environment: A journey to excellence.* Executive summary. Retrieved from http://www.aacn.org/wd/hwe/docs/execsum.pdf

American Association of Critical-Care Nurses (AACN). (2015). *AACN's healthy work environments initiative.* Retrieved from http://www.aacn.org/wd/hwe/content/hwehome.pcms?menu=hwe

Beard, R. (2014, January 20). *Why customer satisfaction is important.* Retrieved from http://blog.clientheartbeat.com/why-customer-satisfaction-is-important/

Centers for Medicare & Medicaid Services. (n.d.). *Hospital Compare.* Retrieved from https://www.medicare.gov/hospitalcompare/search.html

Frampton, S. (2009, March). Creating a patient centered system. *American Journal of Nursing, 109*(3), 30–33.

Herbert, A. A., & Pavel, M. P. (2014). *Random kindness and senseless acts of beauty.* New York, NY: New Village Press.

McLaughlin, J. (n.d.). *What is organizational culture? Definition and characteristics.* Retrieved from http://study.com/academy/lesson/what-is-organizational-culture-definition-characteristics.html

Medicare.gov. (n.d.). *Linking quality to payment.* Retrieved from https://www.medicare.gov/HospitalCompare/linking-quality-to-payment.html?AspxAutoDetectCookieSupport=1

National Institute of Standards and Technology (NIST). (2010, March 25). *Baldrige performance excellence program.* Retrieved from http://www.nist.gov/baldrige/enter/health_care.cfm

Planetree.org. (2014). *Reputation.* Retrieved from http://planetree.org/reputation/

Poh, M. (2014). *5 characteristics of a positive work environment.* Retrieved from http://www.hongkiat.com/blog/positive-working-environment/

Riffkin, R. (2014, December 18). *Americans rate nurses as highest on honesty and ethical standards.* Retrieved from http://www.gallup.com/poll/180260/americans-rate-nurses-highest-honesty-ethical-standards.aspx

Rosenberg, M. (2008, August 19). *Ways leadership affects culture and culture affects leadership.* Retrieved from http://www.humanresourcesiq.com/talent-management/articles/ways-leadership-affects-culture-and-culture-affect/

Seligman, M. E. P. (2002). *Authentic happiness: Using the new positive psychology to realize your potential for lasting fulfillment.* New York, NY: Simon & Shuster.

Seligman, M. E. P. (2011). *Flourish: A visionary new understanding of happiness and well-being.* New York, NY: Free Press.

Sharp. (n.d.). *The Sharp experience.* Retrieved from http://www.sharp.com/choose-sharp/sharp-experience.cfm

8

THE CLOUT OF ALLIES

Holly Jo Langster, DNP, FNP-C, HCA, CENP

OBJECTIVES

- Consider how to build alliances with co-workers and staff.

- Learn to promote teamwork across boundaries.

- Explore how to maximize resources through teamwork.

- Understand the factors that help and hinder positive change.

- Consider the best change process for your organization.

An *ally* is defined as "a person or organization who associates, connects, or unites for some common cause or purpose" (ally, n.d.). Healthcare professionals, and nurses in particular, have a number of opportunities to build allies and connect with others for a common purpose: delivering great patient care.

Building quality relationships takes time and skill. Providing care to patients is "a team sport," and no single provider can do it alone. Miscommunication, misunderstandings, and/or a lack of communication can all produce unintended interpersonal conflict. Conflict causes stress. In some cases, it is unnecessary if the care providers attend to building solid relationships and establishing clear lines of communication.

BUILDING ALLIANCES

Healthcare facilities across the nation have varying elements of team building or teamwork: negative, positive, and somewhere in between. Nurses have a great deal of influence. They often do not give themselves the credit they deserve. As the most present members of the healthcare team, nurses plays a leading role. Nurses facilitate teamwork among many care providers. Nurses also are used to taking an active role to lead teams of diverse individuals. However, nurses are not always on an even playing field, respected for their expertise, or allowed to fully participate as an equal partner in care delivery. The following story offers an illustration.

WHEN WEDGES BETWEEN EMPLOYEES ENCOURAGE MISCOMMUNICATION

Still relatively new, a nurse was reviewing electronic medical records (EMR) of patients who were admitted the previous evening. A newly deployed care model included completing admissions with a multidisciplinary team. The nurse was assessing the records for completeness and accuracy, adding consults as needed, ensuring quality measures were implemented, communicating with the admitting nurse, and encouraging follow-through on any missing elements. The nurse noticed that one heart failure patient did not have an echocardiogram and was not on a beta blocker. She then placed a "sticky note" on the chart for the bedside nurse. The EMR system had one color of sticky notes for nurses and a different color for medical providers. Apparently within the next few hours, one of the care providers on the team (a pharmacist) obtained more information about the patient's status. He appropriately added medications to the list, which included a beta blocker noted in a previous visit. However, he did not remove the sticky note.

The nurse caring for the patient received a phone call from the cardiologist, who proceeded to tell her that she was never to leave notes for any of his patients. He went on to say that he knows his quality measures, he is the best in meeting them, and he didn't need any help from her. He also said he saw the note and thought the patient might have been rehospitalized for not taking a beta blocker. Once he saw the medication list, even he was confused. He then proceeded to tell her she did not know about medications, and if she was too stupid to know them, she should not be commenting on the list.

The nurse tried to explain the new care model and the purpose of the note. Dr. Cardiologist stated he was not interested in the nuances of the process change and cut off the nurse's sentences as she was speaking. He continued to condescendingly accuse her of not knowing the patient's medications. Finally, he got quiet and the nurse simply said, "I hear you." He was silent for only a moment, repeated it all again, and then hung up.

The nurse cried because Dr. Cardiologist made her feel incompetent in her new role. She was also angry because he called her personal cell phone, and she knew that he could only get the number by asking someone in nursing for it. She felt betrayed by her colleagues, and, in her mind, the nurses were all gathered around the nurses' station laughing at how Dr. Cardiologist had just chewed her out.

Fortunately, the nurse felt better as time in the role passed. She later received a surprise phone call from the chief medical officer letting her know that Dr. Cardiologist had been to see him. She was instructed not to make him angry anymore—without even hearing her side of the story.

This story's ending is unfortunate, but it is not all that uncommon. Bad behavior among and between healthcare providers does exist and can cause a great deal of unnecessary stress in the environment. Being a nurse and taking care of sick patients is enough stress without layering on more from behavioral anomalies. However, as nurses learn to avoid the pitfalls relative to ineffective communication or gaps in communication, healthy and positive alliances can be formed. It is wise to build strategic alliances with others before they are needed. Then, once "the going gets tough," nurses have those on the team they can rely on for assistance.

Some call building alliances at work "networking" or "creating good karma" (Schindler, 2014). Schindler advised that it's never a bad idea to create connections with people who you can help and who might be able to help you; the reasons are pragmatic besides just being a nice person. Nurses are usually nice people and generally easy to get along with. Repetition of good communication practices builds trust. People know what to expect from one another. Allies might even become friends. Figure 8.1 shows how trust is the foundation for building alliances.

Figure 8.1 Without trust as the bedrock, you can't build alliances and reap all the benefits.

- Consider doing something nice or helpful for someone else before you need something yourself.
- Share new information when you receive it.
- Work to improve the communication process with teammates.

FORGING TEAMWORK ACROSS BOUNDARIES

The opposite of trust is fear. Teamwork is built on a foundation of trust. It is perfectly acceptable to view trust as an iterative process, waxing and waning at different times. Teammates need to know what to generally expect from each other; time in a specific environment and consistent experience with others contribute to the development of trust. Teamwork is built on trust, and trust is built on transparent communication. Inconsistency in performance creates distrust and the feeling of never knowing what to expect.

Healthcare leaders need to advocate for healthy work environments that exude transparency, open communication, and effective collaboration. Proactive planning for optimal teamwork is critical to organizational success and patient safety. A culture of questioning should be the norm. Any time you face an uncertain situation or unfamiliar order or task, ask questions. A safe environment embraces teamwork, encourages questions, and facilitates learning. When a nurse does not ask necessary questions, it may be a symptom of a bigger organizational or cultural problem.

The culture of an organization is directed by the leadership, whether the leaders intend to direct it or not (Martin, 2006). Cultural anomalies, challenges, and barriers are commonly found in most organizations. Barriers can be invisible to others and can be "covert," such as seat selection or preference in a meeting, what to do while a medical provider is making rounds, or where to sit at the nursing station. Cultural norms can be deeply embedded where everyone knows unwritten rules; some behaviors may be overt in exuding power and authority to undermine teamwork. Behaviors opposed to building effective alliances or teamwork can also be found in organizations, such as bullying and lateral violence. Both silence individuals and groups; neither should be tolerated by leadership in nursing and healthcare. The culture should be transparent and solely patient-focused.

Why might you be afraid to ask a question? Rohde (2015, p. 3) supports problem-solving in high reliability organizations and spoke about the need to review organizational problems and sort the "what" of a problem from the "why" of a problem. Only when we understand why problems occur can we fix them. Otherwise, we cannot fix what might be the problem. Nurses have to feel comfortable asking the right questions. One responsibility Nance (2008) noted of highly reliable organizations is that they create environments that are safe places to ask questions. Asking a question should never be an obstacle; it should be an expectation.

Healthcare needs to globally adopt a helping culture and exude a service orientation. Organizations that simply get by and practice mediocre service will be a thing of the past. Consumers of healthcare have become purchase-savvy. Technology has enabled patients to access information and make educated decisions about where they will receive the best care.

Good practices build trust and trustworthy organizations; just as organizations build trust, so must nurses. Nurses must be consistent in delivering quality communications to provide valid, important information that allows teammates to do their best work. Consistency in communication makes nurses trustworthy; trust builds teams and forges alliances.

MAXIMIZING RESOURCES TO CHANGE THE CULTURE

Culture change is hard work and requires a change in thinking. Organizations must start by assessing the possibilities and then drive change to maximize resources. One of the most commonly used change theories in nursing is Lewin's theory of change. It speaks of unfreezing, changing, and refreezing, and it can aptly be applied to most any situation.

Lewin's (1948) change strategies follow a three-step process that is familiar to most people. It has been popular since the late 1940s and early 1950s. It has three steps, as follows:

- **Unfreezing:** Lewin stated in order for change to occur, the current equilibrium must change. Lewin calls this process *unfreezing.* It is a time for building trust and helping everyone recognize the need for change. Lewin refers to a need for thawing attitudes and using the thaw or unfreezing time to identify problems (the "whys"). Then, engaging in creative problem-solving comes easier to develop solutions or fixes for the problem.

- **Changing:** The second phase of Lewin's change theory is about *moving.* This is a simple yet clear directive. Moving tells the change agent exactly what to do. Move and make the change! This can mean a multitude of different things to different people. As a nurse working to improve teamwork, it may mean move out of your comfort zone and open up your world to include the team around you. Start slowly by adding other nurses to your team and let teamwork develop around you to get through the day. Begin to engage other disciplines and build interdepartmental teamwork.

- **Refreezing:** The last phase of Lewin's change theory is the pre-dictable yet surprising *refreeze.* It is amazing to think that we might want to freeze anything in this world of fast-moving change. It seems that we might require a more "stay on your toes" final phase, knowing that change will most likely be required again. However, refreezing is a necessary step because it is the fol-low-through; it is required for the change to stick. Process changes frequently require policy changes and follow-up audits to evaluate the success of the change (Sullivan & Decker, 2001).

Leaders can use Lewin's theory to assist with organizational change, and nurses can use it to design and implement local change within the immediate work environment. Peer-led change (started by one brave person) can become a change largely recognized by and adapted in a unit or department. When successful, it can be easily spread among peers or be replicated in other areas. This type of communication and change has the potential to go viral in an organization, especially when it is led by the people, for the people.

DRIVING VERSUS RESTRAINING FORCES

Lewin is known for a "change concept," which he calls a *driving force*. Driving forces are those that push us in a direction that encourages or facilitates change. A nurse seeking to make improvements in his/her practice strives to achieve change, and this can be viewed as a driving force. Outcomes-focused payment reform is a driving force. When organizations and providers no longer receive reimbursement because patient outcomes are not reaching the acceptable thresholds, a driving force exists.

Money is often the most stimulating driving force an organization can use to push change forward. This strategy works particularly well when engaging medical-provider behavioral change. When trying to instill change among peers, a driving force can be the biggest complaint existing in a unit. This could be something as broad as "we never have enough staff" or "we don't have the correct supply."

Nurses can be a driving force by thinking back to the engrained nursing process and asking the right questions about "why." Answering questions about "why" and "what are the causative factors" will provide evidence to drive conclusions. The answers to these questions provide clarity about processes that might need focused attention. Identifying a work process or project that requires change is an excellent opportunity for a team to begin to relate to each other as they work through the issue. Identifying potential solutions, performing controlled experiments, and navigating the change process together builds goodwill among team members.

Restraining forces are those that counter the driving forces (Kritsonis, 2005). Dr. Cardiologist and his reluctance to allow nursing involvement in the quality monitoring process would be a restraining force. Any time there is barrier to the progress of change, there is a restraining force. Leadership can indirectly promote restraining forces rather than driving forces when they utilize authoritarian or autocratic leadership styles. These styles of leadership are often intended to be very positive as the leaders work toward providing clear directives and ensuring everyone understands the objectives.

Unfortunately, when the style of leadership is not adjusted (situational leadership) to the growing knowledge of the group, autocratic or authoritarian styles become negative. Creativity, group dynamics, and group influence are often rejected, and employees begin to feel that their input or opinions are without worth.

Thus, employees quickly stop driving forward and begin to revert to the status quo. This reversion to reflect and "complete the task list, clock out as soon as possible" attitude of work ethic is detrimental to organizational culture. Visionary, coaching leadership styles tend to encourage nurses to rise to a high level practice for participation in process change and improvement. Participatory and inspirational leadership is necessary for true, impactful change; it is the essence of teamwork. There is no substitute for the power of one—change can start anywhere, and each nurse needs to think of himself or herself as a leader. It is important for the nursing profession to embrace change and embark on a journey of excellence as healthcare is changing.

Equilibrium exists when driving forces become equal with restraining forces and no change occurs (Kritsonis, 2005). Dr. Cardiologist stopping the nurse in her tracks and deterring her continued monitoring of records for potential errors had the potential to create equilibrium, with no change at all. Many nurses complain about always having to start something new at work. Often they start something new, and within a few weeks or months revert back to the old way of doing things without ever having achieved what the change was intended to achieve. Sustainability for change is difficult, takes focus and hard work, and needs constant review and monitoring. It is nearly always worth the effort.

PRACTICE PEARLS

- Learn to use the concepts of change to facilitate cultural change: driving forces, restraining forces, and equilibrium.
- Become a disruptor to the status quo!
- Help others and begin to seek their support in return.
- Be grateful.

THE CHANGE PROCESS

It is not unheard of to strongly believe in something and have complete buy-in of the need for change but not be able to achieve the change. Weight loss is a perfect example. Many attempt it, but it is difficult to sustain behavior and lifestyle changes. Most everyone understands how to lose weight, but they can't lose the weight or keep it off. Weight loss is hard. It requires a great deal of focus and constant work, it requires preparation and planning, and it requires dedication. Similarly, sometimes change does not succeed because the circumstances necessary to achieve change are simply not present.

Organizational change can be the same way. A healthcare entity can have the best participative leadership, the best-paying patients, kind providers, the easiest electronic medical record system, and a great spirit of teamwork. However, if all of the nurses were educated at the same school and they have not been taught proper practice, clinical outcomes might suffer. Although this is an extreme example, which would most likely never occur, it does make the point. Nurses can sometimes be their own worst enemies. It takes great leadership to create a culture of open and honest transparency, encouraging nurses' participation in problem identification and resolution to promote positive change. Nurses are smart people, and once nurses understand the need for change, they almost always are willing to participate in the change.

Good teamwork can decrease communication frustration and enhance the patient-care experience for everyone while increasing the efficiency and efficacy of provided care. Finally, include the patient in decision-making. As with any major objective, improving patient outcomes requires buy-in from the person whose outcome is being measured. In this case, it happens to be the patient.

MOVING BEYOND NURSING

In the bestselling book titled *Good to Great* (2001), Jim Collins explained why good is the enemy of great. Organizations that are built for excellence typically achieve it. Organizations that are good, even really good, at what they do can rarely reach greatness. Greatness requires a conscious decision by brave leaders to move forward, where merely good organizations are satisfied with the current status. Often, greatness comes from the work of just a few. While it may be amazing to work for a great organization, nurses have the power to influence the ability to become a great unit inside of a good organization.

Cole and Cole (2005) cited the most important elements of teamwork in a four-legged table model—communication, cooperation, trust, and respect. They are each discussed next:

- **Communication:** A must-have when it comes to teamwork. Every team has a leader, whether formal or informal, and that leader must be a great communicator. The same is true in healthcare. Any leader unable to communicate clearly, appropriately, or confidently may remain a leader by position but will not retain the respect of a following.

- **Cooperation:** Great communication plus cooperation yields teamwork. In healthcare, people rely on one another for their expertise. This ultimately benefits the patient. The national scope and standards of practice in nursing lists collaboration as a standard element of teamwork. It states:

  > "The registered nurse collaborates with the healthcare consumer, family, and others in the conduct of nursing practice…partners with others to effect change and produce positive outcomes through the sharing of knowledge of the healthcare consumer and/or situation." (O'Sullivan et al., 2010, p. 57)

  Collaboration is part of nurses' standard of professional practice and is synonymous with cooperation. Collaboration doesn't mean not standing up, compromising ethical standards, or skirting evidence-based practice. Cooperation is not being a "yes-man," but rather, being a "why-man" (or woman).

- **Trust:** This is perhaps the most important part of the four-legged table. Trust is the main support or foundation. Without it the relationship, system, or project might tumble. As previously noted, trust is the opposite of fear. There are not many people in this world who thrive on fear. What is often ignored in healthcare cultures are the silent acts of interaction (or a lack thereof) that break trust in workplace teammates. Elvis sang the song "Suspicious Minds," which said:

> "We can't go on together with suspicious minds, and we can't build our dreams on suspicious minds."
> (James, 1968)

This philosophy also applies to healthcare, because trust is vital to an organization's success; it is the foundation of teamwork. An excellent example of trust established between leaders and staff is found in a shared governance model. Shared governance creates a framework for a healthy work environment that allows nurses to embark on serious organization-wide procedural change, and for all the right reasons. A shared governance organization encourages and supports evidence-based suggestions for improvement and supports change.

- **Respect:** This is the final leg of the teamwork table. It does not have to be present for teamwork to exist, but it does have to be present for proactive teamwork to exist. Respect is a noun, which means it is a *thing*. It's a feeling or an emotion. Respect is how a nurse feels about others and how others feel about him or her. The actions a nurse takes on a daily basis can show respect. The responses a nurse exhibits can show respect. The support a nurse provides can show respect. Not showing respect is most often an act of omission, a passive-aggressive display of disapproval of another person's character, or is exhibited by what a person does or does not value. Finally, respect is common human decency.

Respect is displaying proper manners, exuding kindness, and recognizing equality. Together, healthcare providers can build alliances among diverse groups of people who have the potential to achieve amazing things. Nursing is at the core of this positive progression.

PRACTICE PEARLS

- Never withhold information.
- Always give accurate information.
- Admit mistakes and apologize.
- Be open to feedback.
- Make decisions based on what is best for the greater good.
- Do what you say and say what you will do.
- Be honest and listen attentively.

CONCLUSION

Healthcare organizations of the future need to change the accepted norm in social or workplace culture. Any gathering of employees—including daily huddles, break room gatherings, social gatherings such as hospital picnics or tailgate parties, staff meetings, and leadership updates—are important venues to communicate a new message of radical culture change. You should grasp every opportunity to reinforce the expected behaviors (open and honest communication, respect, transparency, and so on) that promote healthy alliances, teamwork, and ultimately good care and patient safety. It has been said (although no one really knows by whom) that a person must hear something seven times to remember it. Employees bathed in a message of positive culture will eventually get "clean." The next chapter explores quality and safety in relation to stress, fatigue, and burnout.

REFERENCES

ally. (n.d.). In *Dictionary.com*. Retrieved from http://dictionary.reference.com/browse/ally

Cole, L., & Cole, M. (2005). The teamwork values statement. *People smart leaders*, p. 43. Winchester, VA: Oakhill Press.

Collins, J. (2001). *Good to great*. New York, NY: HarperBusiness.

James, M. (1968). "Suspicious minds" [single]. New York, NY: Scepter Records.

Kritsonis, A. (2005). Comparison of change theories. *International Journal of Scholarly Academic Intellectual Diversity, 8*, 1–7. Retrieved from http://qiroadmap.org/download/phase/.201%20Resources/Kritsonis

Lewin, K. (1948) *Resolving social conflicts: Selected papers on group dynamics*. Gertrud W. Lewin (ed.). New York, NY: Harper & Row.

Martin, M. J. (2006). "That's the way we do things around here": An overview of organizational culture. *Electronic Journal of Academic and Special Librarianship, 7*(1). Retrieved from http://southernlibrarianship.icaap.org/content/v07n01/martin_m01.htm

Nance, J. (2008). *Why hospitals should fly: The ultimate flight plan to patient safety and quality care*. Bozeman, MT: Second River Healthcare Press.

O'Sullivan, A., Barcott, J., Bonalumi, N., Collins, S., Darling, L., Davis, G., … Diamond Zolnierek, C. (2010). Standards of professional performance. *Scope and standards of practice: Nursing* (2nd ed., p. 57). Silver Spring, MD: Nursesbooks.org.

Rohde, K. (2015, April 10). Occurrence reporting: Building a robust problem identification and resolution process. *Arkansas Patient Safety Conference*. Lecture conducted at the Arkansas Organization of Nurse Executives (AONE) and Arkansas Association for Healthcare Quality (AAHQ), Little Rock, AR.

Schindler, E. (2014, May 23). Building alliances at work: Getting help before you need it. *The fast track: Tools to get the job done fast*. Retrieved from http://quickbase.intuit.com/blog/2014/05/23/building-alliances-at-work-getting-help-before-you-need-it

Sullivan, E., & Decker, P. (2001). *Initiating and managing change*. In Sullivan, Decker, & Jamerson (Eds.), *Effective leadership and management in nursing*. (p. 250). Upper Saddle River, NJ: Prentice Hall.

9

PLANNING INTENTIONAL QUALITY AND SAFETY

Suzanne Waddill-Goad, DNP, MBA, RN, CEN
Holly Jo Langster, DNP, FNP-C, HCA, CENP

OBJECTIVES

- Consider how intentionality affects workplace decisions and stress.

- Consider how to manage patient risk.

- Explore reliability science.

- Understand the nurse's role in intentional quality and safety.

- Explore how to influence state and national policy.

WHAT IS INTENTIONALITY?

Our first experiences with intentionality are typically in school. Although our parents intentionally feed us, care for us, and play with us for bonding purposes, there is very little agenda-driven interaction to guide the encounters. When we get to school, things are different. Most likely, this is one of the first places we learn about the consequences of feeling stress.

There might be a test to pass at the end of the week, and we have to learn primary colors, count to 10, and be completely bathroom independent in order to advance from preschool to kindergarten. Epstein (2007) speaks about the importance of intentional teaching, which does not happen by chance. It is *planful* (full of plans), thoughtful, and purposeful. Intentional teachers use their knowledge, judgment, and expertise to organize learning experiences for children. When an unexpected situation arises (as it always does), these teachers can recognize a teaching opportunity and are able to take advantage of it, too.

Being an intentional teacher requires a wide range of knowledge and a recognition that learning occurs sometimes from adult-guided experiences and other times from child-guided experiences (Epstein, 2007). Epstein (2007) lists the characteristics of an intentional teacher as: having high expectations, planning and managing, valuing a learning-oriented classroom, offering engaging activities, posing thoughtful questions, and providing feedback. Choosing a career in nursing and the healthcare industry allows practitioners to experience each of these characteristics as learners in the field and then subsequently as care providers.

As adults, most of our learning comes from life experiences. Any formal education we receive is often hand-selected to meet the intentional plan we have for our lives. The word *intentional* is much like the word *purposeful*. In the best-selling book, *The Purpose Driven Life*, Rick Warren notes that what we pay attention to in our lives flourishes. If we nurture sadness by refusing to leave the house or rejoin society after the death of a spouse, we might spiral into a deep depression. If, on the other hand, we nurture friendships that offer support after the death of a spouse, we build stronger relationships and process grief more effectively (Warren, 2002).

Success in life's various elements, whether career, family, faith, physical, or emotional health, is rarely incidental. Success most often comes from intentional planning and attention to detail. Nurses must have intentional focus when it comes to providing care for patients. Nurses naturally and intentionally strive for high quality and optimal safety to help patients achieve the best outcomes. To be intentional is to be purposeful, focused, and determined. Nurses who are unable to focus and prioritize will struggle with higher levels of stress throughout their careers.

Much like learning an instrument, you must practice a little bit every day to retain enough information to be able to advance the selected skill (Warren, 2002). Nursing is a career with many opportunities for practice, learning, and growth. You can change specialties, learn new skills, practice in a variety of work environments, and receive formal advanced education. Being bored is not an excuse for burnout in nursing; opportunity to advance in the profession of nursing is abundant for nurses who are willing to stretch themselves.

Hospitals and healthcare organizations that achieve national notoriety for stellar outcomes in quality and safety are organizations that place intentional focus on those elements, as evidenced by their efficient systems and organizational design.

In an interview with Saint Joseph Hospital West in Lake Saint Louis, Missouri, the chief nursing officer (CNO) was asked, "How does your organization achieve a 'Truven Top 100 Hospital' ranking so consistently?"

She simply replied, "We did not even know we were on the radar for recognition. We simply work to ensure quality and safety are the best that they can possibly be" (Pestle, 2014).

This is an excellent example of intentional focus for the right reason. St. Joseph Hospital West was not only successful in meeting the objective it set out to achieve (excellent quality and safety), but it earned the hospital national recognition. Intentionality can be powerful.

PRACTICE PEARLS

- Be intentional about learning new knowledge and skills.
- Learn to realistically prioritize short-term work to be done each day and longer-term career goals.
- Focus.

PATIENT SAFETY AND TRANSPARENCY AND MANAGING PRACTICE RISK

Many organizations strive to attain a culture of safety. The World Health Organization (2015) provides patient safety organization (PSO) campaign resources such as safe surgery, the safe childbirth checklist, clean your hands campaign, and so on. The Joint Commission seeks to identify how safe an organization is by asking specifically what the facility does to promote patient safety. State hospital associations have devised patient safety organizational programs that are open to hospital participation.

Nurses need to be aware of the variety of national and regional quality and safety programs. Healthcare organizations are expected to make the environment as safe as possible. Because nurses are the vast majority of healthcare providers in most organizations, nurses must clearly understand and apply quality and safety concepts. Applying these to our work environment is done through policy, standardized protocols, and efficient work processes; these create a structure to make the care we provide more reliable.

The era of focus on safety in healthcare began in 1999 with the Institute of Medicine (IOM) report titled, "To Err Is Human." Intimate details about operations and the business of healthcare not putting patient safety first or as a top priority were included. Per the 1999 report, medical errors caused between 44,000 and 98,000 deaths in hospitals each year. Deaths from medical errors are those defined as "could have been prevented" (Kohn, Corrigan, & Donaldson, 2000, p. 1). With the national release of this information, healthcare providers have been vigilant to promote—with clear intention—the prevention of medical errors.

INTENTIONAL PLANS AND CHECKLISTS

In an exposé comparing healthcare to aviation, John Nance (a former pilot and attorney) describes why hospitals should fly. The ultimate flight plan must include intentional systems designed to prevent error (Nance, 2008). A patient-safety orientation and quality care delivery must be precise elements in safe practice. In aviation, Nance described how checklist protocols are applied to standard work processes. The same philosophy could be applied to the variation existing in current healthcare systems. Step-by-step process protocols decrease the need to memorize or recall every step of a process in an emergent situation. Having to remember a great deal of information at a moment's notice can in itself be very stressful, and checklists can relieve that stress.

Although PSOs are often organizations coveted by non PSO-hospitals across the nation, nurses in those facilities can identify with significant pressure for near-perfect performance. The implication that an organization has achieved a foolproof system (to prevent errors) can lead nurses to fear reporting errors that do occur. Nurses must remain vigilant because rarely is any process completely foolproof. The potential for human error cannot be completely eliminated. Being honest about error reporting helps prevent future errors.

PRACTICE PEARLS

- Never rely on memory alone.
- Use "tip sheets" and checklists when possible.
- Patient safety is everyone's job: Be honest and transparent.
- Be intentional about the care you provide; it should be safe and of high quality.

These key strategies are basics to achieving a hospital embedded with a culture of patient safety. "Back to basics" is often a saying used when something goes awry. To solve problems in healthcare, it is imperative to start with the beginning of a process and look at each step along the way for relevance and accuracy. Historically, changes have been applied to current practices or processes without taking the time to break down what currently exists, what needs to change, and what is the best approach to achieving the desired result.

Patient safety organizations frequently utilize the skills of consultants or employees trained in Six Sigma, Lean, or a combination of process-improvement strategies. These specialized skills are an ideal match for organizations who want to improve their safety culture. Participation in process improvement initiatives is a good way for nurses to learn additional problem-solving methodologies.

THE NURSE'S ROLE IN SAFER AND HIGHER-QUALITY SYSTEMS

How do nurses and organizations ensure high quality and safe patient care? Technology can be utilized for building safer systems. Most healthcare facilities now have an electronic health record (EHR). Checklists and standardized protocols can be embedded into the EHR for more consistent decision-making and to reduce practice variation.

One standardized example is that surgical centers and operating suites have nearly universally implemented the safety steps of a "time-out" checklist (approximately a decade ago). Before a procedure begins, a series of questions are discussed among the surgical team. The information is generally entered into the medical record, which only allows the user to proceed if all safety checks and balances have been completed. This standardization has prevented many medical errors, which include wrong-site surgeries, incorrect procedures or anesthesia, and incorrect patient-procedure matches. Following this type of checklist can be simple and it is important; following it step-by-step every time ensures a more predictable and safer outcome.

Each person who chooses a career in healthcare must understand his or her role in patient safety; no position should be exempt. Many organizations conduct daily safety meetings, either in person or via technology. This approach communicates the importance of patient safety and leader responsibility; it also ensures accountability as departments or disciplines are required to report their status. Because healthcare organizations are not silos, each department/discipline influences or has the ability to affect the functions of others.

Safety is everyone's job. If we notice breaks in protocol, such as a lack of hand washing, not labeling specimens in the presence of a patient, or an incomplete timeout, healthcare providers need to be able to speak up. Each person needs to understand the importance and his or her responsibility and needs to feel empowered. For example, a surgeon seen wearing a surgical mask in the hallway outside of the surgery department should be reminded to remove the mask. If a co-worker does not wash his or her hands per protocol, it should be brought to the person's attention. Cultures that support safety also support civility, where all staff are seen as equal team members regardless of rank, position, or tenure.

CREATE A CULTURE OF TRANSPARENCY

A culture of safety in healthcare is evolving. Most institutions are experiencing significant change, and the culture is moving toward improved quality and higher system reliability. Transparency for doing the right things right is becoming the norm—not changing systems or practice solely due to regulatory requirements or intervention. In an organization that's truly encompassing patient safety, everyone knows that everyone else is and will be responsible for achieving a unified goal—safety.

Patient safety is also a primary focus of the U.S. government relative to healthcare. As a result, systems such as the Veterans Administration have made necessary changes to access and care. A national news release in April 2014 (Bronstein & Griffin) revealed at least 40 veterans have recently died while waiting for appointments. Alleged secret lists of patients waiting to be seen were not entered into the computerized scheduling system. Subsequently, the patients never received provider appointments. In addition, no official records existed to indicate a delay in care. Clearly, equal responsibility for patient safety was not infused nor adopted throughout the organization. Transparency was not valued; all realms of the organization, including the operators and receptionists, were not empowered or held accountable to ensure quality and safety were paramount.

MANAGE THE HANDOFF

An additional area of practice risk is the patient "handoff" process. It is a very important element of patient care designed to deliver intimate details of a patient's situation and care requirements and to allow communication between caregivers. Patient care may transition from one provider to another in a variety of situations. Typical handoffs include receptionists, clerical personnel, nurses, medical providers, diagnostic personnel such as laboratory and radiology, and consultative personnel such as a dietitian or a specialist of another discipline. Handoffs may occur either inside an organization or outside to other clinics or facilities. It is incredibly important that handoffs be standardized, be pertinent to individual patient needs, and include safety and quality concerns relevant to their care.

PRACTICE PEARLS

- Be transparent.
- Follow organizational policy.
- Use unique patient identifiers and include the patient in handoffs.
- Share information the next provider needs to know.

BEDSIDE REPORTING

Nursing "report" is a type of handoff or communication process that has historically been in place between nurses. When viewing old movies with hospital scenes, medical records are often seen hanging on the footboard of the hospital bed; this promoted bedside conversations about care and report from nurse to nurse. Since that time, a variety of options for more confidential nurse reporting has evolved, whether in person, by audiotape, or in writing. More recently, report has changed location (moved to the bedside) and includes the patient.

Publications outlining the specific benefits of bedside reporting have been prevalent since the early 1980s. In 1995, Minick published a qualitative study identifying bedside report as a means for critical care nurses to identify potential problems earlier in the care of the patient. Bedside report also resulted in what Minick (1995) deemed "making a connection" with the patient when patients are included in the process.

Implementing bedside reports in an organization that has utilized alternative methods can be quite challenging. It requires a different type of thinking from nurses and new skills in communication. Nurses who have not experienced this style of open communication with patients and/or family members may be unsure of themselves, uneasy with the honest dialogue, and fearful of potential questions. There is no definitive conclusion as to why resistance to bedside reporting exists, but it does (Agency for Healthcare Research and Quality [AHRQ], 2015).

Challenges for nurses to overcome when using bedside report include how to deal with sensitive information in front of a patient, potential violations of confidentiality and privacy, fearing change, and not wanting to disturb the patient (AHRQ, 2015). Changing the process for nurse reporting can be complex. It is very important for nurses and nursing leadership to be jointly involved in planning the change process. The end product must ensure delivery of pertinent information and allow time for quality conversations. Measurement milestones to follow up and evaluate the new process are necessary in order to achieve a successful change in reporting practices.

The literature is rife with studies of organizations implementing bedside report, the challenges of doing so, the processes used, and the benefits reaped. The Agency for Healthcare Research and Quality (AHRQ) published an implementation handbook for bedside report in conjunction with the U.S. Department of Health and Human Services (2015). The step-by-step guide gives clear direction for organizations to begin the implementation process and provides case studies from hospitals that have achieved successful implementation. It also summarizes the benefits of bedside shift report including improved patient satisfaction and less time required to complete the shift report. You can read more about the Nurse Bedside Shift Report at http://www.ahrq.gov/professionals/systems/hospital/engagingfamilies/strategy3/index.html.

Anderson and Mangino (2006) reported improved relationship-building among nurses and improved patient satisfaction; most patients want to know more about their health status and the plan for their care. Caruso (2007) found nurses doing bedside report were frustrated with the repetition of history in front of the patient. Caruso (2007) suggested use of Lewin's change theory when presenting and promoting the concept of bedside report. A new reporting template using only pertinent and current information (with follow-up via mentoring and accountability) worked well for a remodeled bedside report. As a result of the study, nurses continued their improvement work and designed a pre-report that reviewed the patient's history followed by a bedside report for verification of care requirements, as well as the plan for the shift or day. The revised model provided efficiency for nurses and patients.

Many hospitals that try to implement bedside report find frustration among nurses. Because it is a radical change, it is easy to revert to what is more commonly known: nursing station report. Generally, nurses fear failure and especially failure in front of a patient. But is it really fear of the organizational change or the consequences? Whatever the reason, bedside report is best for patient outcomes (Sigma Theta Tau International [STTI], 2012). Both patients and families have reported it improves their understanding of the hospital process and considers needs the patient will have after hospitalization.

The Joint Commission made the second national patient safety goal (NPSG) of 2006 this: *improve the effectiveness of communication among caregivers* (The Joint Commission, 2007). The 13th goal of 2006 was: *encourage the active involvement of the patients and their families in the patient's own care* (Patient Safety Net, 2015). Although The Joint Commission has not specifically listed bedside report as a national patient safety goal, the objectives can be easily met by using the method of bedside report for improved communication. You can read the latest version of The Joint Commission's publication, "America's Hospitals: Improving Quality and Safety: The Joint Commission's Annual Report 2015," at http://www.jointcommission.org/annualreport.aspx.

RELIABILITY SCIENCE AND THE PREVENTION OF HARM

Sheridan-Leos (2014) discussed the premise of *reliability science* as a platform to ultimately improve quality and safety. Historically, reliability science has been commonly used in high-risk industries. The principles are designed to compensate for limitations in human performance, with a movement toward zero defects. Defects in healthcare can be defined as medical mistakes, lapses in service, and other measurable metrics demonstrating quality, safe systems, and operational success. The goals of patient safety intersect with reliability science because they are both intended to prevent harm. Healthcare must develop a laser focus on anticipation of what might go wrong and subsequently design stopgaps to eliminate errors from occurring. The anticipation of error prevention uses systems thinking and change theory; while both concepts are somewhat familiar to nurses, this may be a paradigm shift for some in the ability to see interdependent relationships in complicated processes rather than linear cause and effect (Sheridan-Leos, 2014).

Nurses are vital participants in preventing errors and defects. They are at the "sharp point," or at the point of service (with the customer). Being at the bedside caring for incredibly sick people in trying circumstances is not without risk. However, examples of nursing work processes designed to prevent error include independent verification; individual double-checks; a review of medication side effects; mediation reconciliation; consultation with colleagues regarding policy or procedure standards, and so on. Nurses and organizations that embrace safety science have an opportunity to decrease or eliminate associated organizational stressors resulting from mistakes. Organizational stress often leads to personal stress, which launches the reiterative cycle of stress, fatigue, and burnout.

One of the hallmark characteristics of reliability, as described by Sheridan-Leos (2014)—in the modified definition of Berwick and Nolan's (2003) application of reliability to healthcare—is the measurable capacity of healthcare processes, procedures, or services to perform the intended functions in the required time. Most medical care must be delivered in a timely fashion. Delays in care should be considered a defect. Delays also have the potential to disrupt care delivery and optimal healing as well as the potential to affect outcomes.

Nursing has typically been silent when errors occur in practice. There is an overwhelming fear of litigation and public humiliation of both organizations and individuals who make errors. Honesty takes work. Children do not have to be taught how to lie; they have to be taught how *not* to lie. Natural instincts facilitate protection; protecting ourselves and others is human nature. Living with knowledge that an error occurred is just as stressful as reporting an error and fearing the consequence. Stress, fatigue, and burnout frequently occur more quickly for nurses in organizations where honesty and transparency are not supported, appreciated, or encouraged.

Case 1: In 2011, the media reported a story about a nurse in Seattle, Washington, named Kimberly Hiatt who made a serious medication error (Aleccia, 2011). Nurse Hiatt recognized the error and immediately reported it to the nurse in charge. The child who received the inaccurate dosage of medication had been a frequent patient at the healthcare facility due to a heart defect. The patient did eventually die, but it was never clear if the medication error contributed directly or indirectly to a further decline of the patient's heart function.

As sad as this death was, another unnecessary death occurred subsequent to the investigation. Hiatt had been an employee and worked in her specialty for 24 years and had never knowingly made a critical medication error. After this error, she was thoroughly investigated, terminated from her position at her hospital, and fined by the Washington State Board of Nursing. In addition, the Board of Nursing required her to complete 80 hours of medication administration coursework, and as an additional sanction, she received a 4-year probationary period that required regular reporting. Unfortunately, the shame of the error, the fear of never working again as a nurse, and the guilt of the harm she may have inflicted led her to commit suicide. Hiatt's suicide was just one week after the State Board's ruling.

Case 2: In Ohio, also in 2011, pharmacist Eric Cropp was sentenced to 6 months in jail for the death of a 6-year-old cancer patient. In Cropp's case, he was obligated to supervise a pharmacy technician who inadvertently used the wrong percent of saline while mixing a medication in solution. Unfortunately, Cropp is now a convicted felon and lost his license to practice pharmacy (Lebowitz & Mzhen, LLC, 2011). Healthcare is serious business; inadvertent mistakes can result in unintended death or harm.

Case 3: A temporary nurse was working in an intensive care unit (ICU) and assigned to a critically ill patient. The nurse was new and unfamiliar with the unit and also with many of the hospital's unique protocols. In the absence of an intravenous (IV) pump, standard practice was to use a tube feeding pump to infuse the medication (incidentally, this was in the late 1980s—long before the global focus on patient safety). Against her better judgment, the nurse hung a 250cc bag of dopamine to be used to augment the patient's blood pressure. Unbeknownst to the nurse, shortly after initiation, the tubing became dislodged inside the pump. Later, as the nurse was performing an assessment of the patient, she noticed the arterial line wave form had become very large and accentuated on the monitor, as well as a change in patient condition—the patient had become very restless. As the nurse proceeded to investigate the cause for a change in condition, she looked up and noted that the entire bag of IV medication had run in (through the patient's central line) in a "free-flow" fashion. She was mortified! Next, she immediately notified the nurse in charge and the medical provider. Fortunately, the patient did not suffer any long-term ill effects and was treated with other supportive medications until the dopamine's effects were diminished. However, as for the nurse—she had a very difficult time with the fact that she had made such a potentially grave error. She took a break and went to a private area. There, she had a complete breakdown. She then requested to leave her shift for the rest of the day. The leaders obliged. She had never made a medication error before to her knowledge. The next 15 hours were agonizing for the nurse replaying the scenario in her head, asking herself what she could have done differently, and so on. This story had a happy ending—the medical director of the ICU asked the hospital and the nursing agency for the nurse's contact information. He made a call to the nurse to console her and asked her to come back to work later that day (the call was on the day following the error). He assured her that she could do it and that this mistake should not deter her confidence in her ability to practice nursing in the future! The nurse did go in to the hospital that day to find a very supportive group of clinical colleagues waiting for her return—they allowed her to help them care for patients that day and not be assigned a patient or patients of her own. This compassionate and caring approach made all the difference in her own "recovery" by allowing time to process and finally accept the error. Fortunately, she was able to continue her practice working in this and other ICUs. She has never forgotten the error, and overall, it has made her a better nurse—more present and aware.

No professional curricula adequately prepares future healthcare practitioners with all of the competencies necessary to deliver quality healthcare (Morris, Otto, & Golemboski, 2013). Nurses must take special care to remain vigilant to prevent errors. Strategies for safe practice must include following organizational policy, delivering patient-centered care on an interdisciplinary team, knowing the standards of practice, utilizing available technology, staying current with medical and nursing evidence (practicing evidence-based nursing), being present and aware, and caring for one's own well-being. Providers in healthcare are diligently working to bridge the gaps in the care continuum for improved quality of care. The comprehensive care continuum now includes what happens before an episodic office visit or hospital encounter and those activities that take place inside a hospital, clinic, provider office, and the home environment of patients to ensure care is consistent and meets the patient's needs.

Organizational transparency is necessary to forge optimal safety, quality, and legal reform. Public reporting has removed the veil of secrecy organizations have enjoyed; no longer is there an impenetrable shield when errors occur. Smart organizations have begun to open their private world to the public by bringing together patients, family, healthcare providers, and community members as collective advocates for system change. The objective is to allow participation in setting organizational policy and decision-making by those whom healthcare is designed to serve.

PRACTICE PEARLS

- Learn about reliability science.
- Apply the principles of reliability science to improve quality and safety in the work environment.
- Attend to your own well-being to be able to provide safe care.
- Design or redesign care systems to be safer and more patient-focused.

PROMOTING ACCOUNTABILITY

Promoting accountability is a difficult and somewhat ambiguous task. As people, we often link the words *accountable* and *guilty*; if you are accountable, you are the one to blame. Nurses are generally altruistic people who honor the truth. Telling the truth means reporting errors and catching near misses. Unfortunately, nurses cannot eliminate human error and are subject to error potential with even the most well-designed processes and systems. Making any kind of mistake causes stress. Depending on the gravity of the error, the stress can be extreme, as evidenced by the earlier professional practice examples in this chapter.

Lyons, Adams, Woloshynowych, and Vincent (2004) reviewed a variety of levels of human errors in healthcare, from the most unintentional of absent-minded errors to the intentional maleficent causes of harm. Fortunately, intentional harm is uncommon in healthcare. Typically, human reliability assessment and process improvement efforts within an organization can prevent unintentional errors from recurring.

Dr. Lucian Leape from the Harvard School of Public Health first briefed the U.S. congressional subcommittee on the management of human error in healthcare on October 12, 1999 (Marx, 2001). Leape reported that only 2% to 3% of major medical errors are reported through hospital reporting structures. He stressed the urgency of finding ways for healthcare organizations to prevent errors, eliminate punitive error-reporting responses, and use the errors to improve the chances that they would not be repeated.

Marx (2001) described *disciplinary system theory* as a way to define categories of error based on historical court cases, jury decisions, and penal codes. Errors are then categorized as one of "four evils":

- *Human error*—The one committing the error should have done something other than what he did.

- *Negligent conduct*—Failure to exercise expected care and should have been aware.

- *Reckless conduct*—Conscious disregard of substantial and unjustifiable risk.

- *Knowing violations*—Knowingly violated a rule or procedure.

Similarly, categories of error are used in the decision-making process titled *Just Culture*. The visual model shown in Figure 9.1 outlines the types of error, considerations resulting from investigation of the error, and appropriate follow-up behavior.

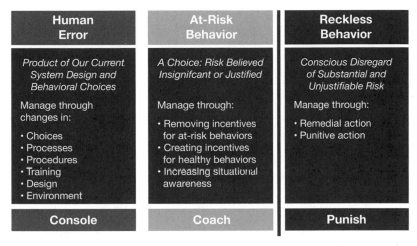

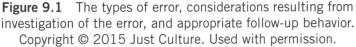

Figure 9.1 The types of error, considerations resulting from investigation of the error, and appropriate follow-up behavior. Copyright © 2015 Just Culture. Used with permission.

Just Culture is a process by which organizations can evaluate errors and determine appropriate responses. The organizational enticement to such a process is that by using the well-designed tools, leaders can encourage more reporting, learn from mistakes without blame, and appropriately identify those who behave recklessly and need to be removed from the organization. Brunt (2010) described how using Just Culture pushes organizations to make six major changes:

- Move from looking at errors as individual failures to realizing they are often caused by system failures.

- Move from a punitive environment to a just culture.

- Move from secrecy to transparency.

- Move from provider-centered care to patient-centered care.

- Move from models of care that rely on independence to models of care that encourage interdependent, collaborative, and interprofessional teamwork.

- Move from top-down accountability to universal and reciprocal accountability.

The visual model shown in Figure 9.2 is supported by learning systems, justice, and accountability. It outlines a cycle of improvement based on values and expectations, which drive system design and behavioral choices, which result in good or bad outcomes.

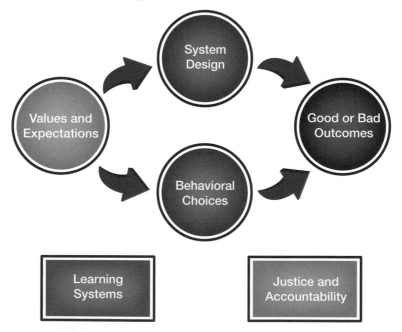

Figure 9.2 The cycle of improvement is based on values and expectations that drive system design and behavioral choices. Copyright © 2015 Just Culture. *Used with permission.*

REPORTABLE QUALITY MEASURES

Using reportable quality measures to drive successful change is something healthcare organizations should strive for. Providers across the nation are being held responsible for reportable quality metrics such as clinical core measures, state-initiated quality indicators, and national patient satisfaction percentile rankings. Additional measurement schemes relative to patient experience and outcomes (patient satisfaction with care, hospital readmission rates, procedural complications, and infection rates for organizations by cause) complicate payment and reimbursement systems.

Decisions have become complicated for patients when selecting healthcare providers. Organizations that are able to convey their quality, safety, and excellent patient experiences will have clientele. Those with poor results will struggle in the marketplace. Organizations that can teach nurses how their individual practice affects fiscal health will be successful. Nurses must learn and understand reportable and reimbursement-dependent indicators. Organizations of the future must build team-oriented cultures with creative talent and use proactive plans to drive quality outcomes. You can learn more about core measures at these two websites:

- http://www.jointcommission.org/core_measure_sets.aspx

- https://www.cms.gov/Regulations-and-Guidance/Legislation/ EHRIncentivePrograms/Recommended_Core_Set.html

Healthcare organizations must eliminate blaming and eliminate sayings such as, "if the physician would only…" or "if the nurse had…" or "it was the cardio-pulmonary staff's fault for not…." Studies show open-ended and honest discussion about errors not only improves communication among the members of the healthcare team but also improves patient care and doesn't lead to increased litigation (Stewart et al., 2006). Organizational stress, fatigue, and burnout are less likely to occur in transparent organizations, where all levels of healthcare providers know what to expect from each other and from the organization.

LEADING INNOVATION AND IMPROVEMENT

Nurses must take the lead to guide healthcare to a better future. Nurses provide the preponderance of care in most if not all types of healthcare organizations. Nurses spend the most time with patients and families. Nurses have significant influence with patients and families in care planning, accepting, and translating treatment recommendations, and understanding the intricacies of their healthcare encounters.

Nursing leadership plays a significant role in the outcomes of patients. Nurse leaders control the resources—the people, places, and things that provide care. The role of a nursing leader, at whatever level, is to set the tone. Nursing leaders must lead by example. Leaders might be in formal positions to set policy and design or collaborate in creating a philosophy for practice or in determining how a shift might operate; they may also have more informal influence as evidenced by everyday dealings with colleagues.

Clinical nurses need to take every opportunity to present themselves as leading the care team: taking charge of care coordination, rounding with other clinical and non-clinical disciplines, thinking of better ways to do things, and monitoring all patient-education initiatives. While medical providers determine the plan of treatment or appropriate procedures for a medical condition, nurses are the communication conduit among team members and the patient for understanding the "what" and the "why."

Participating in evidence-based practice councils and shared governance committees allows nurses to be a part of the important decision-making. Nurses can build the confidence needed to lead innovation and care improvement from these types of activities. Nurses need to be active in the profession and knowledgeable about their chosen specialty. The best patient advocates are informed.

PRACTICE PEARLS

- Volunteer for learning opportunities—stretch yourself.
- Participate in organization-sponsored knowledge-building programs.
- Become an expert.

A healthy nursing culture is critical for both nursing satisfaction and patient experience. In 2013, Sheryl Sandberg (Facebook's COO) went on a crusade to educate women in leadership roles. The vast majority of nurses are women. Sandberg described learned detrimental behaviors by women in corporate culture: They tend to sit in the second row of a meeting room, lack confidence, and are quiet and do not interrupt "testosterone driven" conversations. Women favor being pleasers, kind hearts, and servants (Sandberg, 2013). The same could be said for nurses, and it is time for change.

Nurse leaders must be well educated, experientially prepared, and use their expertise by having a voice. It is time to "sit up and lean in," as Sandberg describes, to become part of the decision-making body. Nurses represent the largest group of employees in healthcare. Nurses do have influence. Nurses can guide organizations to achieve desired outcomes.

It is time for nurses to stand up, take charge, and be a positive force in the healthcare industry.

Nurses must also share their good work. Best practices are routinely discovered in nursing units within organizations every day. Many nurses provide exceptional care and do extraordinary things. Informal research is conducted by daily experimentation to achieve solutions to common problems. Nurses want to practice with high standards. Differing models of care are explored, knowledge is shared between novices and experts, and leadership is abundant. Knowledge is power, and communication is the only way to unleash it.

Most nurses are required to obtain pertinent continuing education to relicense or recertify. However, studying what is new in the literature related to healthcare economics, policy, or innovative methods of care provision can be difficult. The amount of information can be overwhelming. Streamlining subjects or sharing information among colleagues can be effective methods to stay current. Communication among care providers is very important for patient care and for good practice.

Patients are also encouraged to speak up and be involved in their care for their own safety. You can read more about The Joint Commission's Speak Up campaign at these websites:

- http://www.jointcommission.org/speakup.aspx
- http://www.jointcommission.org/assets/1/18/SpeakUp_Poster.pdf

- What kind of communicator are you as a nurse? Do you speak up when it's important and helpful to do so?

- Do your colleagues think you're a valuable participant?

- Are you able to understand the preferences of different generations, cultures, and religions?

- Are you able to understand the finite nuances of disease?

- Can you apply the latest knowledge and research to patient situations?

CREATING A BETTER WORKPLACE

Research shows employee satisfaction can be linked to customer satisfaction or, in healthcare, to the patient experience. Improvements can be low or no cost. The patient experience is a critical component to the assessment of quality. Folkman (2013) listed seven ways one company found to increase employee satisfaction without giving raises:

- Consistent core values exhibited by the leadership that do not disappear during times of stress

- Long-term focus promoting a positive and bright future

- Local leadership accepting feedback and driving change

- Continuous communication in good and bad times

- Collaboration with others to maximize resources and teamwork

- Abundant opportunities for development

- Speedy and agile decision-making

Nurses are the backbone of any healthcare operation; the influence they possess must not be wasted. Nurses must be active participants in improvement activities and take full advantage of the perks associated with employment, such as tuition reimbursement, certification pay differentials, and educational offerings. Being a good employee requires give and take. More than a decade has passed since the first report by the IOM regarding the status of safety in healthcare. We can do better. Being an involved employee in an environment devoted to quality and safety provides a buffer from organizational stressors.

Staying connected to purpose buffers stressful conditions. In Pistorius's 2013 book *Ghost Boy*, he described a nurse who loved her job. She performed her duties with passion and commitment every day. As a result, she saw life in the boy who was truly alive inside his prison of a body. The patient, named Martin, had a mysterious illness causing him to be comatose. He lost all bodily functions, including speech. However, one day his mind woke up but he couldn't let anybody know. Virna, his nurse, took time to relate to the boy as if he were awake. She didn't know if he was actually "in there" or not. In doing so, she found life in a boy and gave him a great gift (Pistorius, 2013). Virna was not stressed by the patient's condition or the environment, but instead provided him with care, compassion, and human kindness.

PRACTICE PEARLS

- Why did you become a nurse? Passion and purpose provide amazing individual and professional rewards.
- Stay involved and contribute by sharing what you know.
- Always give your best.

INFLUENCING STATE AND NATIONAL POLICY

Nurses are ideal advocates for healthcare change. Their knowledge and expertise of what is best for patients cannot be matched. Nurses must remain abreast of current issues to be informed and vote on amendments and healthcare laws with conviction. Be a promoter of health and the prevention of illness. Use nursing and non-nursing related venues as a platform to share expertise. Consider volunteering to speak about nursing and healthcare in the community. Be knowledgeable about the impact of changing healthcare law. The political arena offers a number of opportunities for nurses to get involved in driving change: testifying, lobbying, and/or running for public office.

Nurses occasionally find themselves in situations of distress. These situations commonly challenge their patience, integrity, and values. It can be morally distressing to seek justice or what you believe to be the best care for a patient without having the plan supported or agreed upon by the patient, the family, or in some cases even the medical provider. Worldwide challenges remain, such as, impoverished people and/or communities with no means of obtaining or growing their own food are not likely to have healthy food choices. Religious communities with strict conviction about immunizations may require specialized provisions to help fend off viruses and/or disease.

Many social issues still exist in nursing and healthcare both inside and outside of the United States. Often, these types of challenges are shared with nurses and can be a source of stress. Conflicts arise in healthcare as they do in any other industry on a regular basis, but in healthcare and nursing, the conflict may have a direct impact on someone's life. Thus, a stronger focus on quality and safety must be included in all plans for the future of nursing and healthcare.

CONCLUSION

What is nurtured is what will flourish. O'Reilly (2009) pronounced that healthcare was slightly improving 10 years after the IOM report on errors. The progress has been slow, and experts in the industry would give the effort toward safety and quality a grade ranging from a B– to a C+ (O'Reilly, 2009; Wachter, 2010). We can do much better. We can manage patient risk, improve safety, and become more reliable in what we do. Ask yourself these questions:

- What are you nurturing in your practice?

- What are your organization's leaders nurturing?

- What is your community nurturing?

- What can you do in your practice to make a difference?

The next chapter discusses strategies to reduce stress and fatigue in an effort to banish burnout and to promote a healthy work-life balance.

REFERENCES

Agency for Healthcare Research and Quality (AHRQ). (2015). *Nurse bedside shift report implementation handbook.* Retrieved from http://www.ahrq.gov/professionals/systems/hospital/engagingfamilies/strategy3/index.html

Aleccia, J. (2011, June 27). Nurse's suicide highlights twin tragedies of medical errors. NBC News. Retrieved from http://www.nbcnews.com

Anderson, C., & Mangino, R. (2006). Nurse shift report: Who says you can't talk in front of the patient? *Nursing Administration Quarterly, 30*(2), 112–122.

Bronstein, S., & Griffin, D. (2014, April 23). A fatal wait: Veterans languish and die on a VA hospital's secret list. CNN. Retrieved from http://www.cnn.com/2014/04/23/health/veterans-dying-health-care-delays

Brunt, B. (2010, May 18). Developing a just culture. *Healthleaders Media.* Retrieved from http://healthleadersmedia.com/page-1/NRS-251182/Developing-a-Just-Culture

Caruso, E. (2007). The evolution of nurse-to-nurse bedside report on a medical-surgical cardiology unit. *MedSurg Nursing, 16*(1), 17–22.

Epstein, A. (2007). *Introducing intentional teaching: Choosing the best strategies for young children's learning.* Washington, DC: National Association for the Education of Young Children.

Folkman, J. (2013, November 27). Seven ways to increase employee satisfaction without giving a raise. *Forbes.* Retrieved from http://www.forbes.com/sites/joefolkman/2013/11/27/seven-ways-to-increase-employee-satisfaction-without-giving-a-raise

The Joint Commission. (2007). Improving American hospitals: A report on quality and safety. Retrieved from http://www.jointcommission.org/improving_americas_hospitals_the_joint_commissions_annual_report_on_quality_and_safety_-_2007/default.aspx

Just Culture. (n.d.). *Getting to know just culture.* Retrieved from https://www.justculture.org/getting-to-know-just-culture/

Kohn, L., Corrigan, J., & Donaldson, M. (2000). *To err is human: Building a safer health system.* Washington, DC: The National Academies Press.

Lebowitz & Mzhen, LLC. (2011, November 16). Pharmacist jailed for fatal medication error. Retrieved from http://www.marylandinjurylawyer.net

Lyons, M., Adams, S., Woloshynowych, M., & Vincent, C. (2004). Human reliability analysis in healthcare: A review of techniques. *The International Journal of Risk and Safety in Medicine, 16,* 223–237.

Marx, D. (2001). *Patient safety and the "Just Culture": A primer for healthcare executives.* Retrieved from http://www.safer.healthcare.ucla.edu/safer/archive/ahrq/FinalPrimerDoc.pdf

Minick, P. (1995). The power of human caring: Early recognition of patient problems. *Scholarly Inquiry for Nursing Practice: An International Journal, 9*(4), 303–317.

Morris, S., Otto, C. N., & Golemboski, K. (2013). Improving patient safety in healthcare quality in the 21st century: Competencies required of future medical laboratory science practitioners. *Clinical Laboratory Science, 26*(4), 200–204.

Nance, J. (2008). *Why hospitals should fly: The ultimate flight plan to patient safety and quality care.* Bozeman, MT: Second River Healthcare Press.

O'Reilly, K. B. (2009, December 28). Patient safety improving slightly, 10 years after IOM report on errors. *American Medical News.* Retrieved from http://www.amednews.com/article/20091228/profession/312289980/6

Patient Safety Net. (2015). The role of the patient in safety. U.S. Department of Health and Human Services; Agency for Healthcare Research and Quality. Retrieved from https://psnet.ahrq.gov/primers/primer/17/the-role-of-the-patient-in-safety

Pestle, J. (2014, January 1). [personal interview].

Pistorius, M. (2013). *Ghost boy.* Nashville, TN: Nelson Books.

Sandberg, S. (2013). *Lean in: Women, work, and the will to lead.* New York, NY: Knopf.

Sheridan-Leos, N. (2014). Highly reliable healthcare in the context of oncology nursing: Part 1. *Clinical Journal of Oncology Nursing, 18*(2), 151–153.

Sigma Theta Tau International (STTI). (2012). Nursing handoff at the bedside: Does it improve outcomes? Virginia Henderson Global Nursing E-Repository.

Stewart, R., Corneille, M., Johnston, J., Geoghegan, K., Myers, J., Dent, D., … Cohn, S. (2006). Transparent and open discussion of errors does not increase malpractice risk in trauma patients. *Annals of Surgery, 243*(5), 645–651.

Wachter, R. M. (2010). Patient safety at 10: Unmistakable progress, troubling gaps. *Health Affairs, 29*(1), 165–173. Retrieved from http://content.healthaffairs.org/content/29/1/165.full.html

Warren, R. (2002). *The purpose driven life: What on earth am I here for?* Grand Rapids, MI: Zondervan.

World Health Organization. (2015). *Patient safety campaigns.* Retrieved from http://www.who.int/patientsafety/campaigns/en/

10

PROMOTING WORK-LIFE BALANCE

Suzanne Waddill-Goad, DNP, MBA, RN, CEN

OBJECTIVES

- Explore the state of the nursing profession in terms of stress and burnout.

- Consider what you can do to mitigate stress and burnout at your place of work.

- Consider how your choices affect your stress level, good and bad.

- Learn healthy coping strategies from the experts.

- Consider whether stress really is harmful or not.

A REVIEW OF BURNOUT

Maslach and Leiter (2005) have both studied and measured burnout in numerous populations and settings over the last several decades; burnout is a chronic problem. In order to reverse the trend, researchers believe burnout is not a problem for individuals to solve; rather, burnout is a problem of the social environment in which they work. Furthermore, when organizations do not recognize the human side of work in workplace interactions, including how work is completed, and do not assess if mismatches exist between the nature of the jobs and the people, there is a greater risk of burnout (Maslach & Leiter, 2005).

The paramount risks of burnout are both professional and personal. Maslach and Leiter (2005) describe six areas for person-job mismatches:

- **Workload:** Too much work and/or not enough resources
- **Control:** Micromanagement, lack of influence, and accountability without power
- **Reward:** Not enough pay, acknowledgment, or satisfaction
- **Community:** Isolation, conflict, and disrespect
- **Fairness:** Discrimination and favoritism
- **Values:** Ethical conflicts and meaningless tasks

They describe personal consequences that may include a detriment to health and strained private lives; professional consequences may include absenteeism, job hopping, poor relationships with others, and a preponderance to be distracted. One's commitment to work will most likely wax and wane, and in a nurse's case, patients may suffer.

The true cost of burnout in nursing is unknown. These six areas high-lighted by Maslach and Leiter (2005) in the *Stanford Social Innovation*

Review provide valuable organizational insight. A quick assessment by healthcare entities and their leaders may raise awareness to lessen or eliminate the potential for burned-out workers.

Modern nursing is plagued by increasing professional stressors (Smith, 2014). Smith (2014) and McCloskey and Taggart (2010) described that the modern world of healthcare and tightening budgets is resulting in additional work-related stressors such as barriers to providing care, increasing complexity of patient needs, shorter acute episodic lengths of stay, the need for increased knowledge of ever-changing technology, nursing shortages, poor staffing, long work hours, limited resources, and feelings of lack of control. Much of the research in the literature, as well as anecdotal practice findings, are consistent with this description.

Each of the areas described by Maslach and Leiter (2005), when applied to nursing and/or healthcare, could be remedied as follows:

- **Workload:** Reasonable, achievable, and safe

- **Control:** An engaged and involved workforce

- **Reward:** Adequate compensation and recognition for a job well done

- **Community:** A sense of true teamwork and meaningful relationships

- **Fairness:** No discrimination or tolerance of favoritism

- **Values:** An ideal match of aligned passion and purpose

Could enlightened and engaged nurses and nursing leaders, as well as other leaders in healthcare, solve the current dilemma in the social environment of healthcare? The task seems somewhat daunting on a global scale. However, what if one-by-one or entity-by-entity, we began making small changes? Could these changes affect a single department, a single division, a single organization, a single health system, and, eventually, a region, county, state, or country?

THE VALUE OF TIME

All too often in our quest for success, we jostle our way through life, juggling priorities as best as we can. We try to balance all of the competing activities. However, in the hustle and bustle of life, we frequently neglect what matters most—to take time to think or to intentionally plan our lives. One of life's lessons learned as people age is that time is finite—there is only so much of it. It is a habitually overlooked valuable resource to be savored and nurtured.

For example, if you live to the age of 80, that is nearly 22,000 days of adult life. There are approximately 20 to 22 workdays per month, leaving about 8 to 10 days of "free time." However, this does take into account that not much else gets accomplished on a nurse's designated workday (due to the abnormally long hours).

If examined from the perspective of a weekly routine, there are 168 hours of total time available per week. If you work 40 hours per week, sleep 56 hours per week, and spend 10 hours per week on activities related to daily grooming, this leaves a balance of 62 hours per week for commute time, life's activities, and free time. This amounts to a mere 8.86 hours per day. If any of the listed activities encroach on your allocation of time, this 8.86 hours per day suffers and shrinks.

PRACTICE PEARLS

- Consider a time analysis or work sampling project of your life. What do you spend your available time doing?

- Assess if the time spent is doing what you want to do.

- If the exercise shows a gap in what you want for your life, change it.

THE SIGNIFICANCE OF CHOICE

Frequently, others make choices for us. We choose to allow people to guide our future, steal our present, and unearth the past. Much of what causes stress comes from the environment or situations in which we place ourselves, including poor personal relationships, bad work cultures, difficult friends or family, and other life stressors. Consciously, we often think we don't have choices. But don't we? Have we really lost the ability to choose what we do and with whom we spend our time? Can we not make changes to our current circumstances?

Indecision is a decision—good, bad, or otherwise. Of course, sometimes there is value in not deciding. Some conditions change and some problems really do solve themselves. Being thoughtful and present, intentional in your thinking, grounded or centered enough to appraise the options, able to limit and control emotion, and objective when thinking about how you feel are all learned skills that require practice.

In a social sense, society teaches us that being busy equals success. Successful people always seem to be busy. However, being too busy can lead to stress, fatigue, and eventually burnout. What are successful people busy doing? Is what they are doing really making a difference for themselves? Is it making a difference for others? Is their contribution truly of value?

PRACTICE PEARLS

- Think of a person who many people consider successful. What does the person do differently?
- Successful people have limitations and clear boundaries that surround their time.
- Choose wisely—relationships, work, and time spent.

THE FOUR-LEGGED STOOL OF PHYSICAL, EMOTIONAL, MENTAL, AND SPIRITUAL WELL-BEING

What is *well-being*? It is defined as "a good or satisfactory condition of existence; a state characterized by health, happiness, and prosperity" (well-being, n.d.). As previously noted in Chapter 7, Seligman's (2011) positive psychology movement described well-being in terms of "flourishing." Pertaining to healthcare, to *flourish* might be defined as the ability to grow, develop, and/or attract health.

Notably, as people age, well-being tends to improve. Aging is reportedly associated with a positive change in attitude, a greater acceptance of one's physical limitations, contentedness with past accomplishments, reduced preoccupation with peer pressure, and a more realistic appraisal of one's strengths and weaknesses (Jeste & Oswald, 2014). This is excellent news for the majority of practicing nurses, as the average age of nurses is near the midlife or midcentury mark. In addition, most leaders in health are even older, with a large percentage approaching retirement.

Well-being is also reported to be high for those embarking on adult life (Jeste & Oswald, 2014). Jeste and Oswald (2014) reviewed a multitude of studies that commonly show that after the beginning of adult life, well-being seems to decline until about midlife; hence the midlife crisis. Then, well-being continues in an upward trend toward positive well-being on the way to the end of life.

A number of academic sources define spiritual well-being as being very personal; it encompasses values and beliefs that lead to purpose and meaning. Meaningful work does provide purpose. Work is central to most people's lives because it provides income, a sense of meaning and purpose, and a place to build important relationships. Thus, job satisfaction is seemingly a relevant aspect of well-being (Gurkov, Harakova, Dzuka, & Ziakova, 2014).

Although research has been conducted in a throng of industries about work satisfaction, the authors found little evidence in this study to support research related to satisfaction and well-being in nursing or other health-related disciplines. The tool they selected for measurement contained the following elements important to nurses:

- Satisfaction with their work

- Scheduling practices

- Work-life balance

- Relationships with co-workers

- Interactions at work

- Professional opportunities

- Praise and recognition

- Control and responsibility

Interestingly, the researchers' findings did not support the idea that subjective well-being is influenced by job satisfaction, but more importantly, satisfaction with life comes from meaningful interactions and extrinsic rewards. This study reinforces the importance of culture, relationships, and extrinsic rewards. Nurses have the ability to effectively contribute to the development of a positive and healthy work culture and build rewarding relationships, and they possess some ability to influence or affect extrinsic rewards.

For centuries, in a multitude of cultures, age has been associated with wisdom. Jeste and Oswald (2014) defined collective characteristics of wisdom to include social reasoning and decision-making, emotional regulation, insight, contributions to common good, tolerance of diverse value systems, acknowledgement of uncertainty, spirituality, sense of humor, and openness to experiences. Nurses are wise due to their vast experience. This collective definition describes a nurse's role in the promotion of health and healing. Harnessing this wisdom and using it in practice can be the challenge.

Loehr and Schwarz (2003) posited that every one of our thoughts, emotions, and behaviors has an energy consequence, for better or worse. The ultimate measure of our lives is not how much time we spend on the planet, but rather how much energy we invest in the time that we have. Their prescription for success is simple: Performance, health, and happiness must be grounded in the skillful management of energy. Nurses should thoughtfully develop approaches to conserve, preserve, and appropriately allocate portions of energy in the practice of nursing. Stress consumes energy. Proper assessment of physical and mental energy, as well as taking stock of emotional and spiritual well-being, may be crucial to preventing the detrimental effects of stress, fatigue, and burnout.

PRACTICE PEARLS

- Don't be a victim of learn, earn, and burn.
- Design and implement new strategies to become "burnout-proof."
- Live empowered; begin by taking care of yourself first.

HEALTHY COPING STRATEGIES

Common knowledge and learned wisdom show that what we don't schedule doesn't get done. When people get busy, they sacrifice sleep, healthy food, and exercise for other pursuits. Health, well-being, and wellness must become a concern. As nurses age, rest time or recovery becomes increasingly necessary to recharge from the demands of a busy life. Without recovery, the job becomes more difficult, stress causes fatigue, physical and mental tolerance weaken, and these can lead to a host of negative conditions. Time for respite must become the norm, and scheduling time to recover must become important.

In addition to the usual recommendations of getting adequate rest and sleep, eating a balanced diet, and obtaining the recommended amount of physical exercise for optimal health, you should also consider adding deliberate "mental" exercises. Adequate coping strategies allow:

- Individuals an adequate appraisal of stressors

- An appropriate response to the threat stressors present

Numerous studies have investigated the defining characteristics of nurses who ineffectively cope with stress. These include sleep disturbances, interference with relationships, an inability to focus, more illness, and progression to burnout (McCloskey & Taggart, 2010).

RESILIENCE AND HARDINESS

Resilience and *hardiness* are two concepts related to an individual's response to stress. Why can some people become hardy and resilient to life's demands and stressors? The answer: their thinking. Foureur, Besley, Burton, Yu, and Crisp (2013) described an evolution of inquiry relative to resilience that has been organized into three "waves" of study:

- The first wave focused on resilience as a set of characteristics such as hardiness, coping, self-efficacy, optimism, and adaptability.

- The second wave involved the study of resilience as a dynamic process where adversity was met with adaption, secondary to learned behavior or gained experience.

- The third and most recent wave of study defines resilience in terms of an innate energy or a motivating life force within individuals that enables adequate coping via a change in thinking.

MINDFULNESS

The origin of "mindfulness" and most meditative methods can be historically traced back to Eastern Buddhist practices (Hardy, 2015). Sources in the literature describe an emergence in the late 1970s where study and practical application began to surface about mindfulness in western medical and psychological practices. The origin of much of the early research in the United States was in patient populations and was meant to reduce stress; today's multitude of scientific evidence supports this notion.

In recent years, the study of mindfulness has gone mainstream and has become more prevalent in non-clinical populations, including with nurses. Mindfulness training utilizes a variety of meditative practices. *Meditation* encompasses mental exercises and the cultivation of awareness by training the mind to be present (DuVal, 2009, p. 5). Mindfulness training also teaches a set of active regulation skills that patients (or others) practice by themselves in order to cope with medical or stressful conditions (Wylie, 2015).

White (2013) describes key findings from her research about the connection of mindfulness to nursing as:

> "The concept of mindfulness encompasses intricately connected attributes: it is a transformative process, where one develops an increasing ability to experience being present with awareness, acceptance and attention. Mindfulness can support improving physical, emotional, psychosocial and spiritual well-being, and can help translate holistic health promotion from theory to practice. Integrating mindfulness into education and practice can enhance therapeutic nursing qualities and support a shift from a purely theoretical way of knowing to one that is more embodied and holistic."

Dr. Jon Kabat-Zinn is known to be one of the first Western adopters of mindfulness (The Center for Mindfulness, 2014; Kabat-Zinn, 2013). Kabat-Zinn's idea, when introduced, was that mental and emotional acceptance could generate an inner shift in experience that often resembled a cure (Wylie, 2015). Over time, his agenda evolved into what is known today as the *mindfulness-based stress reduction* (MBSR) program, and he has written a number of associated books over the last 35 years to convey his thoughts.

What if nurses could apply the same principle in changing their thought patterns or perceptions of the environment, relationships, and health? In Smith's (2014) review of the literature (to assess the state of science) relative to MBSR as a potential intervention to improve the ability of nurses to effectively cope with stress, she concluded that plentiful benefits exist in utilizing MBSR in the practice of nursing.

We know mindfulness can be trained and is positively associated with measures of psychologic well-being and quality of life (Schoormans & Nyklicek, 2011). Self-improvement seems to be the single golden key to successfully navigating the troubled waters of stress, fatigue, and the potential for burnout in all aspects of life. In addition, *meditation* refers to a family of techniques shown to decrease anxiety and depression by a conscious attempt to focus attention in a non-analytical way and to avoid discursive, ruminating thoughts (Schoormans & Nyklicek, 2011).

Schoormans and Nyklicek (2011) summarize a simple procedure that nurses can follow by engaging in eight sequential steps. This procedure was designed via a working definition of meditation formulated by a collection of experts:

1. Utilize a defined medication technique.

2. Use logic relaxation (letting go of logical thought).

3. Enter a self-induced "state."

4. Move into an aura of psychological relaxation somewhere in the process.

5. Master this self-focused skill or use it as an anchor.

6. Obtain an altered state or mode of consciousness, mystic experience, enlightenment, or suspension of logical thought processes.

7. Embed the context of meditation in a spiritual/religious/philosophy context.

8. Experience mental silence.

Most importantly, taking time for self-reflection can provide a sense of peace and healing. The ability to decrease or change the perception of stress, resulting in less fatigue and less potential to burn out, will yield enhanced well-being and a higher quality of life.

PRACTICE PEARLS

- Learn to be mindful in order to change your thinking.
- Become hardy—hardiness neutralizes stress and buffers reactions to adverse conditions.
- Consider taking mini mental breaks to focus on breathing or "checking in" with yourself about how you feel or find things.

A CONTRARIAN VIEW OF THE IMPACT OF STRESS

Is it possible that stress is actually not bad for us? Could it be positively channeled for a different impact? New information has recently become available that suggests that not all of the effects of stress can be categorized as detrimental. Stress does not necessarily have to be viewed as the enemy. And it is not always a negative antidote to adequate human performance.

There is developing research about mindset, the positive effects of stress, and enhanced performance secondary to a healthy dose of stress in a variety of situations and settings. Mindset science is emerging, and one of the best-known young researchers is Dr. Alia Crum, whose recent work at Columbia University in New York was revolutionary. Her research focuses on how changes in subjective mindsets—the lenses through which information is perceived, organized, and interpreted—can alter objective reality through behavioral, psychological, and physiological mechanisms. Her work is, in part, inspired by research on the placebo effect, a notable and consistent demonstration of the ability of the mindset to elicit healing properties in the body (GoodThink, Inc., 2015).

Crum is interested in understanding how mindsets affect important outcomes outside the realm of medicine, in the domains of behavioral health and organizational behavior. More specifically, Crum aims to understand how mindsets can be consciously and deliberately changed through intervention to affect organizational and individual performance, physiological behavior and well-being, and interpersonal effectiveness (GoodThink, Inc., 2015).

Could there be a gap in healthcare related to mindset? Do healthcare providers have the right thinking about harnessing stress in order to do good in the world in inherently stressful environments? Could their thinking be reframed? In Crum's revolutionary research, she utilized samples of regular people and showed drastic changes of improvement in mindset based on the very same circumstances. Her experiments were designed to show results only secondary to a change in mindset, with no other behavioral or lifestyle changes.

There is the potential if nurses could change their mindset that they could decrease stress, fatigue, and the potential to burn out. Similarly, world-class adventurers adopt a "no-barriers" mindset; this type of mindset encourages community thinking by sharing ideas to achieve challenging goals (Rowden-Racette, 2013). A day in a nurse's life is like an extreme adventure: fraught with unpredictability, uncertainty, and inherent stress. Doing difficult things can challenge your beliefs, and this often requires a change in your mindset in order to be successful.

Mindset is also interconnected with quality and safety. If quality is inherent to doing good work, and healthcare providers want to do good work, why does healthcare not have better results? Sherwood and Zomorodi (2014) described the new science of quality and safety shifting from the prevailing models focused on individual action to a focus on team and system improvements. They also recognized the need for changes in how nurses are educated (trained thinking) to meet the new practice demands. The Quality and Safety Education for Nurses (QSEN) six areas of competency now have knowledge, skills, and attitudinal competences woven into them.

The QSEN competencies encompass all of nursing practice: patient-centered care, teamwork and collaboration, evidence-based practice, quality improvement, safety, and informatics (Sherwood & Zomorodi, 2014). Full engagement and proactive inquiry to develop safe practices are evidenced by a mindset of mindfulness and focused attention. Nurses need to have a calm and confident demeanor or mindset as described by Robotham (2014). This mindset entails learning mind-changing or brain-transformation skills that result in greater mental clarity, physical vitality, and whole-of-life balance.

In the book titled *The Upside of Stress*, McGonical (2015) outlines how stress might actually be good for us and explains how people can get good at using it. Epstein (2015) reminded us that correlation does not imply causation. This is a fundamental lesson in psychology, and violating this principle can lead to serious misconceptions and maybe even dangerous practices. It is easy to draw incorrect conclusions about the causes of stress and the resulting consequences.

Hall (2015) describes six phases to discovering the upside of stress:

1. Be honest about self-talk (acknowledge it, accept it, and move on).

2. Catch it before it starts (identify the stress early).

3. Reframe challenges as opportunities (a change in mindset).

4. Think about what works and does not work for you (identify triggers).

5. Change your surroundings (make lifestyle changes).

6. Ask for help (use available resources).

In addition to the personal consequences of stress, professional penalties may surface. Misperceptions of attitude or capability or incorrect assumptions about motives may limit work-related opportunities. Generally, people like to work with other people they know and like and who are similar to them. Fitting into the right organizational culture and being perceived as positive, enthusiastic, and competent is far better than being seen as negative, burned out, and questionably competent.

Many of the prevalent and most significant health-related conditions today's workers suffer are not caused solely by workplace hazards but also result from a combination of work and non-work factors. These include genetics, age, gender, chronic disease, obesity, smoking, alcohol use, and prescription drug use (Schulte et al., 2015). Nurses and others in healthcare must consider the individual and organizational impact of stressful work. Only then can effective strategies be designed to mitigate the consequences of stress.

PRACTICE PEARLS

- Study the effects of stress, both positive and negative.

- Assess yourself on the Perceived Stress Scale (10 items) at http://www.psy. cmu.edu/~scohen/PSS.html.

- Learn more about mindfulness-based stress reduction (MBSR) at http://www. umassmed.edu/cfm/stress-reduction.

- Find mindfulness meditation tools with Dr. Jon Kabat-Zinn at http://www. mindfulnesscds.com.

- Review the cutting-edge research by Dr. Richie Davidson, who says that well-being is a skill, at http://www.investigatinghealthyminds.org.

Don't forget to have fun—life is short and it seems to pick up speed as we age.

CONCLUSION

What if the stress in nursing and healthcare could be reframed and harnessed as positive? A positive view of stress could change the environment. If nurses and other healthcare providers did not feel stress, at least in the same way, there may be less fatigue and the propensity to burn out. Healthy living is a choice. Not an easy choice at times, but it is a choice. Placing a higher priority on health, with a more reasonable work-life balance, yields a much more satisfying life. The next, and last, chapter brings it all together with a look toward the future.

REFERENCES

The Center for Mindfulness. (2014). *History of MBSR*. Retrieved from http://www. umassmed.edu/cfm/stress-reduction/history-of-mbsr/

DuVal, M. (2009). *Mindfulness based stress reduction handbook*. Knoxville, TN: The Mindful Center.

Epstein, R. (2015, June 11). MIND reviews "The upside of stress." *Scientific American, 26*(4). Retrieved from http://www.scientificamerican.com/article/mind-reviews-the-upside-of-stress

GoodThink, Inc. (2015). *Dr. Alia Crum* [biographical sketch]. Retrieved from http:// goodthinkinc.com/speaking/alia-crum

Gurkov, E., Harakova, S., Dzuka, J., & Ziakova, K. (2014). Job satisfaction and subjective well-being among Czech nurses. *International Journal of Nursing Practice, 20*(2), 194–203.

Hall, E. (2015). *6 simple steps to discovering the upside of stress.* Retrieved from http://www.huffingtonpost.com/2015/02/02/turn-bad-stress-into-good-stress_n_6524954.html

Hardy, S. (2015). Mindfulness: Enhancing physical and mental well-being. *Practice Nursing, 26*(9), 450–453.

Jeste, D. V., & Oswald, A. J. (2014). Individual and societal wisdom: Explaining the paradox of human aging and high well-being. *Psychiatry: Interpersonal & Biologic Processes, 77*(4), 317–330.

Kabat-Zinn, J. (2013). *Full catastrophe living: Using the wisdom of your body and mind to face stress, pain and illness.* New York, NY: Random House.

Loehr, J., & Schwartz, T. (2003). *The power of full engagement: Managing energy, not time, is the key to high performance and personal renewal.* New York, NY: Free Press.

Maslach, C., & Leiter, M. (2005). Reversing burnout: How to rekindle your passion for your work. *Stanford Social Innovation Review, Winter,* 43-49. Retrieved from http://ssir.org/articles/entry/reversing_burnout

McCloskey, S., & Taggart, L. (2010). How much compassion have I left? An exploration of occupational stress among children's palliative care nurses. *International Journal of Palliative Nursing, 16*(5), 233–240. doi: 10.12968/ ijpn.2010.16.5.48144

McGonical, K. (2015). *The upside of stress: Why stress is good for you, and how to get good at it.* New York, NY: Penguin Books.

Robotham, J. (2014). How to create a calm and confident mindset. *Australian Nursing & Midwifery Journal, 22*(4), 30.

Rowden-Racette, K. (2013). The no-barriers mindset. *ASHA Leader, 18*(10), 56–57.

Schoormans, D., & Nyklicek, I. (2011). Mindfulness and psychologic well-being: Are they related to type of meditation technique practiced? *The Journal of Alternative and Complementary Medicine, 17*(7), 629–634. doi: 10.1089/acm.2010.0332

Schulte, P. A., Guerin, R. J., Schill, A. L., Bhattacharya, A., Cunningham, T. R., Pandalai, S. P., … Stephenson, C. M. (2015). Considerations for incorporating "well-being" in public policy for workers and workplaces. *American Journal of Public Health, 105*(8), e31–e44.

Seligman, M. E. P. (2011). *Flourish: A visionary new understanding of happiness and well-being.* New York, NY: Free Press.

Sherwood, G., & Zomorodi, M. (2014). A new mindset for quality and safety: The QSEN competencies redefine nurses' role in practice. *Nephrology Nursing Journal, 41*(1), 15–72.

Smith, S. A. (2014). Mindfulness-based stress reduction: An intervention to enhance the effectiveness of nurses' coping with work-related stress. *International Journal of Nursing, 25*(2), 119–130.

well-being. (n.d.). In *Merriam-Webster's online dictionary.* Retrieved from http://www.merriam-webster.com/dictionary/well-being

White, L. (2013). Mindfulness in nursing: An evolutionary concept analysis. *Journal of Advanced Nursing, 70*(2), 282–294.

Wylie, M. S. (2015). How the mindfulness movement went mainstream – And the backlash that came with it. *Alternet, Psychotherapy Networker.* Retrieved from http://www.alternet.org/personal-health/how-mindfulness-movement-went-mainstream-and-backlash-came-it

11

LOOKING TOWARD THE FUTURE

Suzanne Waddill-Goad, DNP, MBA, RN, CEN
Debra Buck, DNP, MSN, RN

OBJECTIVES

- Explore how to succeed as a nurse in the changing landscape of healthcare.

- Consider how increasing your education and/or knowledge can increase your job satisfaction.

- Learn how technology advances your professional goals.

- Look realistically at how stress affects your job and your life.

PRESCRIPTIONS FOR SUCCESS: EXTERNAL RECOMMENDATIONS

Every nurse should be familiar with the Institute of Medicine's (IOM) report in 2010, called *The Future of Nursing: Leading Change, Advancing Health*. This report was generated as a response to the recognized need to transform the profession of nursing. Four key messages were identified in the report:

- Nurses should practice to the full extent of their education and training.

- Nurses should achieve higher levels of education through a seamless system.

- Nurses should become equal partners with all members of the healthcare team to redesign healthcare in the United States.

- Data collection and information systems should improve to support policy-making and workforce planning.

Could implementation of the recommendations radically change the practice of nursing and decrease stress, fatigue, and the potential for burnout? The only way for nurses to know is to do something different than before. Nurses must learn where change can make a difference and take action.

PRACTICE TO YOUR FULL EXTENT

The first message from the IOM's (2010) recommendations for nurses to practice to the full extent of their education and training implies that nurses are not doing this now. Why not? What barriers are present that prohibit nurses from utilizing their knowledge and skills to the fullest extent?

Ward (2014, p. 1) identified nine common problems in the "very rewarding but equally challenging" practice of nursing:

- **Staffing:** Inadequate resource allocation

- **Interprofessional relationships:** Produce conflict

- **Patient satisfaction:** Many have unrealistic expectations

- **On-the-job hazards:** Related to safety

- **Mandatory overtime:** Due to insufficient resources or high patient acuity

- **"Ask a nurse":** Everyone wants to ask nurses questions about their health issues

- **Patient relationships:** Cause stress, pain, and feelings of loss

- **Advances in technology:** Require changes in duties and skill

- **Certifications and other demonstrations of competence:** Now a must

Similarly, during a BSN completion program titled "Nursing Research" (Buck, 2014), practicing nurses were asked about barriers to implementing evidence-based practice and conducting nursing research. The primary impediment nurses cited was time. The nurses stated that their workload did not allow time for any other activities outside of direct patient care. The nurses verbalized an understanding of the importance of conducting research, and many had taken courses, yet they found it difficult to utilize what they had learned.

It might be time for nursing work to be revamped in the age of pay-for-performance. Analysis of nursing work, just as in building a business case, could yield novel yet drastic recommendations. It is plausible there could be greater returns on investment, better utilization of resources, and improved patient outcomes by radically changing how nurses work.

The second issue prohibiting nurses from practicing to the full extent of their education and training is the inconsistency in practice regulations from state to state. Some states allow a wide scope of practice, with full prescriptive authority for the advanced practice nurse (APN), where others do not. In addition to the variability in the scope of practice, there are also variations in required supervision. In some states, advanced practice nurses can practice independently; in others, they must be either directly or indirectly supervised by a physician as specified in the state's Nurse Practice Act.

If nurses are going to practice to the full extent of their education and training, scope of practice and supervision standardization must occur. The future of nursing rests with the profession to promote the importance of nurses as equal and valuable members of the healthcare team. Through the use of research, nurses will be able to quantify substantive activities as opposed to referring to common successful practices as "it is the way we have always done this." In addition, adopting nursing best practices from research findings will add credibility to practitioners in the profession.

ACHIEVE MORE EDUCATION

The second message presented in the IOM report (2010) was that nurses should achieve a higher level of education and training. This can easily be structured via a seamless system that promotes academic progression. The report calls for 80% of the nursing workforce to have the minimum preparation of a bachelor of science in nursing degree (BSN) by 2020. Although there are many patient-care outcomes that support an all-BSN staff, the majority of nurses currently working in the United States either possess an associate degree or have graduated from a diploma program. As of 2008, only 36.8% of nurses held a bachelor's degree (AACN, 2015). You can read more about nursing statistics at the American Association of Colleges of Nursing's Fact Sheet at http://www.aacn.nche.edu/media-relations/fact-sheets/nursing-fact-sheet.

This change in the required educational standard presents an interesting dilemma. Due to industry financial pressures, many healthcare entities are decreasing or eliminating education reimbursement for those seeking an advanced degree. At the same time, many healthcare entities have decreased or eliminated financial incentives or pay differential for advanced education. Concurrently, some healthcare entities have espoused a course of action requiring a BSN for associate and diploma degree nurses to be completed within 7 years of hire.

An additional hurdle for nurses to return to school is the requirement to repeat courses they may have already taken in entry-level training to meet newer graduation requirements; unfortunately, some course work has an expiration date. Education must be easily accessible and streamlined for nurses to pursue the achievement of a higher degree. Employers must be supportive, with flexible schedules and judicious use of financial resources for support. Education should be viewed as an investment versus a cost, and nurses must be committed to obtaining new skills and education regardless of financial support. Education in nursing does have a return on investment with new opportunities, obtaining a set of qualifications for a higher role, and so on. Grants, loans, and scholarships should all be explored in addition to personal and employer resources.

The IOM report further recommended that the number of nurses prepared at the doctoral level double by the year 2020. In order to achieve this goal, nurses must be vocal regarding their educational needs to be able to complete a higher degree. Fortunately, schools of nursing have become creative in offering varying methods of attaining an advanced degree. This has come largely from the objective of meeting numerical targets for students and consumer demand. Increasingly, online offerings, registered nurse (RN) to master of science in nursing (MSN) programs, and RN to doctor of nursing practice (DNP) programs are budding. As we move into the future, we must place emphasis on the value of an advanced degree and provide support for those seeking such degrees. Even more importantly, we must ensure that nurses can utilize and apply their learned knowledge. Also in 2008, it was discovered that only 13.2% of the nation's registered nurses held either a master's or doctoral degree as their highest educational preparation; the current demand for master's and doctorally prepared nurses for advanced practice, clinical specialties, teaching, and research roles far outstrips the supply (AACN, 2015).

BECOME AN EQUAL PARTNER

A third message from the IOM report (2010) stated nurses should collaborate with physicians and other healthcare professionals as full partners to redesign healthcare in the United States. This is an immense opportunity for collective collaboration and for nurses to have a voice in healthcare's future. This recommendation provides a platform for change in healthcare that can ultimately be patient-focused.

The Affordable Care Act (ACA) of 2010 (or Obamacare as it is commonly called) has radically changed the delivery of healthcare, shifting a greater out-of-pocket expense to many U.S. citizens. Utilizing APNs to provide primary care, standardizing treatment for patients with similar diagnoses, and including the patient in the care process can revolutionize healthcare as we know it. Nurses can champion many of the changes that healthcare needs.

IMPROVE DATA-COLLECTION METHODS

The fourth and final message put forth in the IOM report (2010) identified that effective policy-making and workforce-planning related to healthcare require improved data-collection methods along with an improved information infrastructure. One of the greatest challenges that nurses face is the potential to make an error. Patient deaths due to medical errors ranked third in the top five causes of death, only superseded by heart disease and cancer (McCann, 2014). Nurses' fear of repercussions when reporting an error is one of the most commonly cited reasons for not reporting medical errors (Haw, Stubbs, & Dickens, 2014). In addition, reporting systems can be complicated, many do not allow for accurate near-miss reporting, and some are difficult to navigate.

In the future, it will be essential to identify more efficient ways for nurses to capture real and potential errors. Some organizations have taken steps to internally publicize information about "lessons learned." This is a substantial change in thinking and past practices. Nurses often know patients the best of all other healthcare providers, and they should be leading the way toward enhanced quality and safety initiatives.

In one example of collaboration with other healthcare professionals, the Robert Wood Johnson Foundation took a leap of faith by bringing together a diverse group of people to clarify the role of the APN (Iglehart, 2013). This is what nursing and healthcare need: teams of experts solving complex and long-standing problems. Nurses must have confidence and be willing to share their expertise with others related to care delivery, the practice of nursing, and in the legislative arena.

PRACTICE PEARLS

- Be a team player and recognize the strengths in others.
- Share expert knowledge (gained over time) for improvement initiatives.
- Be willing to learn from others.

PRESCRIPTIONS FOR SUCCESS: INTERNAL RECOMMENDATIONS

In recent times, interpersonal interactions in healthcare settings have become more challenging for nurses. The social environment has been profiled as a source of stress. With a laser-like focus on customer experience and satisfaction, operational performance, and publicly reported metrics, nurses often feel trapped in tough interpersonal situations. A balance must take place with realistic expectations, achievable outcomes, and a safe process to get there.

Customer experience or satisfaction is important. However, care must be taken to meet customer requests without compromising the nurse and/ or his or her better judgment. Nurses are on the front line, taking heavy responsibility for meeting patient, family, and provider needs. In some healthcare settings, if customer needs are not met, the nurse is to blame. Nurses also blame each other.

Cipriano (2015) refers to these types of issues as "emotional labor" in nursing. She defines *emotional labor* as emotions that nurses are required to exhibit such as a smile, a comforting gesture, deference, or scripting when they do not truly feel the emotion. This takes a tremendous toll on nurses, and they often release their stress via frustration and anger with those around them. Peers and subordinates are easy targets. Frequently, there are no obvious repercussions in general for this type of behavior. There is an old saying, "Physician, heal thyself." Nurses also need to consider healing themselves; they are the only ones capable of changing the circumstances in the profession of nursing.

In a recent exchange with an ED (emergency department) nurse, she shared a brief conversation that took place between her and an administrator. The nurse had taken care of a patient in the ED who was a member of a local gang. She shared her concern related to the safety of the staff in the ED based on a recent string of gang shootings in the city. The patients were brought to her hospital, and the gang member told her that the biggest safety concern the hospital should have is the ED waiting room windows.

He described that gang members often drive through the parking lot to see who is in the waiting room. The waiting room's windows allowed anyone sitting in the area to be seen. The nurse was mortified and immediately took this information seriously by reporting it to the hospital administration as a safety concern. The response from the administrator a few days later was, "the interior decorator did not feel it would be aesthetically pleasing to frost the glass," so they had no intention to further address the issue.

Safety needs to be at the highest level of concern in healthcare, including work safety, patient safety, and healthcare-provider safety. Nurses need to assess and report areas of risk—understanding fully that others may not see an immediate need for change. Be convincing! Job safety includes injuries that occur secondary to lifting; slips, trips, and falls; a lack of proper equipment; and is potentiated by working long hours and rotating schedules. Nurses are at risk for injury, so supplies and equipment need to be operational and readily available to provide care.

Lachman (2014) described how The Joint Commission issued a Sentinel Event Alert (in 2008) that addressed behaviors undermining a culture of safety:

> "Intimidating and disruptive behaviors can foster medical errors, contribute to poor patient satisfaction and to preventable adverse outcomes, increase the cost of care, and cause qualified clinicians, administrators and managers to seek new positions in more professional environments." (The Joint Commission, 2008)

Yet, these types of behaviors are still tolerated in a number of healthcare settings. Research shows an increase in lateral violence; bullying; violence in the nursing work environment from patients, visitors, and physicians; as well as increasing mental and emotional demands by the plethora of information available in the literature. *Lateral violence* refers to acts that occur between colleagues, where *bullying* is described as acts perpetrated by one in a higher level of authority and occur over time; the acts can be verbal or nonverbal aggression (American Nurses Association [ANA], 2011). *Horizontal violence* refers to a relationship in a reporting structure where one person is subordinate to another and may experience these types of unprofessional behavior.

In one case during a 7-day period, 12.1% of ED nurses experienced an act of physical violence, and 42.5% experienced verbal abuse (Emergency Nurses Association [ENA], 2011). The acts of violence were committed by patients and visitors. Perpetrators of verbal abuse included peers and medical providers, as well as patients and visitors. The ENA also noted that organizations with reporting mechanisms related to these types of incidents have significantly lower numbers of acts of violence within the organization (2011). Training for nurses (as well as all other healthcare providers) to recognize, dissuade, and prevent violence in health settings is crucial.

Nurses' idealism and professionalism can be undermined by individuals who create unhealthy or even hostile work environments (Lachman, 2014). This type of work culture is problematic to survive in and causes a great deal of stress. Lachman (2014) cites a range of examples of disruptive behavior including throwing objects, banging down the telephone receiver, intentionally damaging equipment, exposing patients or staff to contaminated fluids or equipment, bullying, and lateral or horizontal violence.

Lateral or horizontal violence can be overt, covert, or both. Stanton (2015) describes how nurse leaders must take an active role to eradicate it. There is no place for this type of behavior in healthcare settings, and zero tolerance should be the mantra of the future. In addition to leadership, all nurses must be educated on the signs of lateral violence and be assertive in their ability to communicate to intervene (Ceravolo, Schwartz, Foltz-Ramos, & Castner, 2012). Behaviors include gossiping, withholding information, and ostracism (ANA, 2015).

Positive mentoring is an underutilized role in nursing. The potential benefits are well documented in the literature (Green & Jackson, 2014). Having a "wingman" or a "buddy" to support newbies, those changing specialties, those learning new roles, and so on can be invaluable. Mentoring can have a strong impact in peer-to-peer interactions. Novice nurses need to see good examples of practice, interpersonal relations, and leadership to mold their own style. Mentors serve as a guide. In some organizations, mentors take on the role without recognition or additional compensation. They are frequently asked to work with others in addition to maintaining their own workload. Exercise caution to avoid burning out those interested in mentoring and/or becoming leaders.

Public recognition for a job well done, as well as highlighting positive work contributions of expert nurses is a must; nursing must serve as an example to others, both inside and outside the profession to continue to attract qualified, talented, and dedicated people to healthcare. Caring for each other is an important aspect in nursing that needs heightened awareness. An example is described below, where multiple incidents affect nurses, yet they receive little if any support.

DEALING WITH PERSONAL LOSS IN THE ED

An ambulance is dispatched to a call for a shooting victim. A radio call immediately comes into the emergency department (ED) with situational details. The nurse learns that the patient is a detective from the local police department who is in full cardiac arrest. The ED staff know most members of the police force well due to the small geographic area. Multiple police officers enter the ED as the detective is being wheeled into the trauma room. The staff on duty recognize the detective. The nurses, the physician, and the respiratory therapist take over care from the paramedics. The room is chaotic and emotions are high. After a lengthy resuscitation attempt, the detective is pronounced "dead on arrival." The ED staff leave the room in tears, all the while knowing that they must pull themselves together to continue taking care of the other ED patients who are currently in the department. There is no time for a debriefing.

Later, a debriefing is held for the police officers and the paramedics who were involved. Nursing should have been included—either through an informal (immediately post incident) or formal (days after the incident) debrief. Two weeks after the incident, one of the ED physicians suddenly died at home. The staff were notified by the paramedics on scene (after permission from the physician's wife was obtained). The ED staff, once again, experienced a second and more significant loss, with no formal debriefing. The ED staff knew patient care needed to continue for the other ED patients, so the nurses pressed on.

While this case is somewhat of an extreme example, nurses' experiences are so often overlooked. Nurses are expected to carry on despite feeling grief from troubling events. Nurses need to support each other by advocating for resources to provide needed care at difficult times. A nurse is not just a nurse; nurses regularly take on the role of social worker, chaplain, and counselor in times of crisis. Nurses refer to their peers as "family" due to the traumatic encounters that forge tight bonds. And, in these types of situations, they should be supported like family.

In today's chaotic and stressful healthcare environment, it is vital to recognize the ramifications for nurses of inherent stress, the physical and emotional toll, and the potential for burnout. Nurses can be counted on to do what is necessary under almost any circumstance. Educating the public is an essential piece of nursing's responsibility and helps those outside the profession gain a realistic understanding of the role.

PRACTICE PEARLS

- Don't tolerate bad behavior.
- Recognize feelings and take the time to adapt to them.
- Look out for each other—be a good "wingman."
- Seek help in tough situations.

TYING IT ALL TOGETHER

Technology is changing the world. It is one of the newest and most challenging additions to healthcare; however, it is badly needed to move nursing and the healthcare industry forward. New advances in information technology appear nearly every day. Staying current with the skills required through training, experience, and interaction with others can be daunting. Peers and patients feel the impact of constant change. The implementation of technology is testing both the art and science of nursing. While it should be improving practice, it may be causing additional stress, fatigue, and the potential for burnout due to the excessive amount of change.

The ability to look at a machine to obtain clinical information is nothing short of amazing. However, it may also place nurses' critical thinking skills at risk. Over-reliance on technology for an accurate reading of blood pressure or heart rate, a bar code scanner or pump for medication administration, and other medical device advances may compromise a nurse's ability to effectively solve problems. Critical thinkers in nursing must be skillful in applying intellectual knowledge for sound reasoning (Heaslip, 2008). Nurses must guard their knowledge and maintain the ability to think critically and "just know" when something isn't right.

Heaslip (2008) concluded that nurses must be adept at gathering, focusing, remembering, organizing, analyzing, generating, integrating, and evaluating information. The world is changing the ways we interact with information. More information is available now than ever before. Formal nursing training lays a foundation for critical thinking. However, in practice nurses encounter increasingly more complex situations, which require expert reasoning (Heaslip, 2008). The future of nursing depends on the ability of nurses and healthcare in general to possess new expertise fueled by technology and rapid change, to remain devoted to quality and safety, and to be intentionally thoughtful. We must not lose sight of the human factors that allow nurses to care for themselves, their co-workers, and their patients in an empathetic way.

One of the messages in the IOM report (2010) is the need for nurses to partner with others to improve healthcare. A major contribution to the quality of healthcare for individuals is for nurses to participate in and conduct solo, multi-provider, or specialty research. Nurses have been practicing at the bedside by utilizing differing treatment methods and resources to provide similar care since the beginning of nursing.

One of the biggest challenges nurses of the future will face is the need for new scientific evidence to support practice. In addition, practice environments must become skilled at rapid-fire change so they are able to quickly embrace evidence-based research recommendations for improvement in systems, processes, and procedures. This could potentially change the social milieu.

Hockenberry, Wilson, and Barrera (2006) cited the following reasons as barriers for nurses to make improvements: limited knowledge of the nursing research process, lack of knowledge related to statistics and their use in research, time to conduct and/or implement research, and a lack of power and authority to implement change. Additionally, a lack of respect from peers, decreased resources to provide patient care, poor work environments, and job dissatisfaction continue to contribute to the limited amount of research being appropriated into practice. The time for change is now; nurses can no longer accept the status quo and survive in today's stress-laden healthcare environments.

In addition to the barriers of implementing research at the bedside, there is a known lack of prepared nurses to conduct research. How many healthcare organizations support formal research and development (R&D) programs? Is it considered a core part of their healthcare business (as other industries consider research and development)? How many healthcare entities have a "learning lab" set up to test new ideas or pilot new programs? The numbers are few, unless the healthcare organization is formally aligned with an academic source. Informal research by healthcare providers, in their work environments, is taking place every day in an attempt to do things better. These systems need to be formalized, and new knowledge needs to be shared.

In 2011, the Health Resources and Services Administration estimated the number of nurses with a doctorate at 1% (Nickitas & Feeg, 2011). Doctoral programs in nursing are increasing in the United States, with multiple sites and creative educational formats to allow nurses to obtain the degrees, but there are not enough (American Association of Colleges of Nursing [AACN], 2015; Anderson, 2013). These projections could have a grave impact on the ability to obtain qualified faculty to train new nurses and to conduct necessary research in the future.

A further complication to increasing the number of nurses with advanced educational preparation is the wide gap in compensation. Often, nursing researchers and faculty are paid lower salaries than nurses entering the nursing profession and/or practicing at the bedside. As nursing moves into the future, this needs to change. Nursing needs to keep pace in advancing the profession and stature among other disciplines; higher education is one answer.

One of the most difficult challenges nurses face when speaking up, attempting to make improvement suggestions, or continuing to advance via educational pursuits is the negative comments by their peers. This lack of collegial support causes unnecessary stress. Alienation from peers by negative comments deters nurses from suggesting organizational improvements and engaging in self-improvement activities. As a profession, nurses must move to embrace compassion and care for fellow nurses. Nurses who serve in leadership positions must be committed to providing necessary support. This type of encouragement and a change in the culture of nursing could facilitate a revolution of positive change.

Ward (2014) identified mandatory overtime and the length of nursing shifts as concerns for nurses and patients. According to Stimpfel, Sloane, and Aiken's research (2012), shifts exceeding 13 hours in length result in proportionately higher patient dissatisfaction. In addition, the combination of shift rotation, working overtime, and continual changes in personnel and staffing create a higher level of stress and turnover, which potentiate fatigue and burnout.

In an interview with Beverly Malone, the CEO of the National League for Nursing (Sullivan, 2014), she stated the future of nursing remains in flux and the following considerations must be taken seriously for nurses of the future: an aging workforce, a lack of educators, and too few new nurses entering the profession to meet patient-care demands. In addition, a lack of relevant research, multiple generations of nurses in the workforce, aging leaders in healthcare, and increasing pressure on healthcare organizations further complicate needed change. As healthcare continues to evolve, many new challenges and opportunities will surface. New roles in nursing will be discovered, care will continue to move to alternative venues, and the demand for advanced practice nurses will grow. Educators and clinicians are predicted to be in short supply. The time is now to design and develop new strategies for nursing's future.

PRACTICE PEARLS

- Get involved—support professional practice and nursing research.
- Engage in self-improvement.
- Recognize the value of advancing knowledge and skill.

CONCLUSION

Nurses have a tremendous responsibility to promote and support a new system of healthcare. Cohesion is necessary for a single voice supporting unified policy and practice. While direct care for patients will remain a priority, supportive elements to deliver care in complex atmospheres will be required. Hopefully, many facets of nursing practice in the future will change for the better: research to policy-making, new evidence regularly implemented in practice, a focus on health and prevention of illness, a shift from stress-laden cultures to those supporting optimal well-being, excellent leadership, and most of all, constructive interactions with each other. It is each nurse's responsibility to promote optimism and engage in mindful practice to ensure that nursing remains the most trusted profession and that we leave a progressive legacy for those who follow.

The concepts, questions, and exploration of topics throughout this book were meant to provoke thought—not necessarily thoughts about how things got to this point, but what we can do differently going forward. Some of the information may be viewed as controversial, not usually discussed, or even intentionally hidden in a veil of secrecy. If we don't change, how can we change nursing and healthcare for the better?

This quote from author, speaker, consultant, and university president, Nido Qubein, seems apropos for healthcare:

> "Your present circumstances don't determine where you can go; they merely determine where you start."

It is time to start a revolution! Positive change is crucial for nursing and healthcare. We must strive to change the environment to banish stress, fatigue, and burnout! Onward!

You can read more about the latest trends in healthcare at these websites:

- http://healthaffairs.org/blog/2015/02/25/top-5-health-care-trends-to-watch-in-2015/

- http://fortune.com/2015/01/14/5-trends-that-will-redefine-your-healthcare-experience-in-2015/

- http://www.modernhealthcare.com/

- http://www.pwc.com/us/en/health-industries/top-health-industry-issues.html

- http://www.healthcareitnews.com/news/top-5-healthcare-it-trends-2015-poised-shake-industry

- http://www.usnews.com/topics/subjects/health-care

- http://www.himss.org/news/

REFERENCES

American Association of Colleges of Nursing (AACN). (2015). *DNP fact sheet.* Retrieved from http://www.aacn.nche.edu/media-relations/fact-sheets/dnp

American Association of Colleges of Nursing (AACN). (2015). *Nursing fact sheet.* Retrieved from http://www.aacn.nche.edu/media-relations/fact-sheets/nursing-fact-sheet

American Nurses Association (ANA). (2011). *Lateral violence and bullying in nursing.* Retrieved from http://www.nursingworld.org/Mobile/Nursing-Factsheets/lateral-violence-and-bullying-in-nursing.html

Anderson, C. (2013, October 11). More nurses with graduate doctoral degrees needed. *Petersons.* Retrieved from http://www.petersons.com/graduate-schools/doctoral-nursing-graduate-degrees.aspx

Buck, D. (2014, April 5). *Evidence-based practice.* Lecture presented at Leadership in Classroom, Battle Creek, MI.

Ceravolo, D. J., Schwartz, D. G., Foltz-Ramos, K. M., & Castner, J. (2012). Strengthening communication to overcome lateral violence. *Journal of Nursing Management, 20*(5), 599–606.

Cipriano, P. (2015, September 19). Mitigating the risks of emotional labor. *The American Nurse, 47*(3), 3.

Emergency Nurses Association (ENA). (2011, November). *Emergency department violence surveillance study.* Retrieved from https://www.ena.org/practice-research/research/Documents/ENAEDVSReportNovember2011.pdf

Green, J., & Jackson, D. (2014). Mentoring: Some cautionary notes for the nursing profession. *Contemporary Nurse: A Journal for the Australian Nursing Profession. 47*(1/2), 79–87.

Haw, C., Stubbs, J., & Dickens, D. (2014). Barriers to the reporting of medication administration and near misses: An interview study of nurses at a psychiatric hospital. *Journal of Psychiatric and Mental Health Nursing. (21)*9, 797–805.

Heaslip, P. (2008, revised). *Critical thinking and nursing.* Foundation for Critical Thinking. Retrieved from http://www.criticalthinking.org/pages/critical-thinking-and-nursing/834

Hockenberry, M., Wilson, D., & Barrera, P. (2006). Implementing evidence-based practice in a pediatric hospital. *Pediatric Nursing, 32*(4), 371–377.

Iglehart, J.K. (2013). Expanding the role of advanced nurse practitioners: Risks and rewards. *The New England Journal of Medicine, 386*(20), 1935–1941. doi: 10.1056/NEJMhpr1301084

Institute of Medicine (IOM). (2010). *The future of nursing: Leading change, advancing health.* Washington, DC: National Academies Press. Retrieved from http://books.nap.edu/openbook.php?record_id=12956&page=R1

The Joint Commission. (2009, July 9). *Sentinel event alert, issue 40: Behaviors that undermine a culture of safety.* Retrieved from http://www.jointcommission.org/sentinel_event_alert_issue_40_behaviors_that_undermine_a_culture_of_safety/

Lachman, V. D. (2014). Ethical issues in the disruptive behaviors of incivility, bullying, and horizontal/lateral violence. *Urologic Nursing, 35*(1), 39–42.

McCann, E. (2014, July 18). Deaths by medical mistake hit records. *Healthcare IT News.* Retrieved from http://www.healthcareitnews.com/news/deaths-by-medical-mistakes-hit-records

National Council of State Boards of Nursing (NCSBN). (2015). *Nurse practice act, rules & regulations.* Retrieved from https://www.ncsbn.org/nurse-practice-act.htm

Nickitas, D. M., & Feeg, V. (2011). Doubling the number of nurses with a doctorate by 2020: Predicting the right number or getting it right? *Nursing Economics, 29*(3), 109–110, 125.

Stanton, C. (2015). Action needed to stop lateral violence in the perioperative setting. *AORN Journal, 101*(5), 7–9.

Stimpfel, A. W., Sloane, D. M., & Aiken, L.H. (2012). The longer the shifts for hospital nurses, the higher the levels of burnout and patient dissatisfaction. *Health Affairs (Project Hope), 31*(11), 2501–2509. doi: 10.1377/hlthaff.2011.1377

Sullivan, K. (2014, September 25). *The future of nursing: An industry in flux.* Retrieved from http://www.fiercehealthcare.com/special-reports/higher-education-and-nurse-educators

Ward, J. (2014). *9 common problems in the nursing profession.* Retrieved from http://www.nursetogether.com/9-common-problems-nursing-profession

INDEX

D

E

F

O

P

From the Honor Society of Nursing,
Sigma Theta Tau International

The *Nurse's Advantage* Series

The Nurse's Etiquette Advantage, Second Edition

Kathleen D. Pagana

The Nurse's Grantwriting Advantage

Rebecca Bowers-Lanier

The Nurse's Social Media Advantage

Robert Fraser

The Nurse's Communication Advantage

Kathleen D. Pagana

Sigma Theta Tau International
Honor Society of Nursing®

nursing **KNOWLEDGE**
international®